Berlitz®

Nor

phrase book & dictionary

Berlitz Publishing
New York   London   Singapore

No part of this book may be reproduced, stored in a retrieval system, or transmitted in any form or means electronic, mechanical, photocopying, recording, or otherwise, without prior written permission from APA Publications.

Contacting the Editors
Every effort has been made to provide accurate information in this publication, but changes are inevitable. The publisher cannot be responsible for any resulting loss, inconvenience or injury. We would appreciate it if readers would call our attention to any errors or outdated information. We also welcome your suggestions; if you come across a relevant expression not in our phrase book, please contact us at: **comments@berlitzpublishing.com**

All Rights Reserved
© 2018 Apa Digital (CH) AG and Apa Publications (UK) Ltd.
Berlitz Trademark Reg. U.S. Patent Office and other countries. Marca Registrada. Used under license from Berlitz Investment Corporation.

Thirteenth Printing: May 2018
Printed in China

Editor: Helen Fanthorpe
Translation: updated by Wordbank
Cover Design: Rebeka Davies
Interior Design: Beverley Speight

Picture Researcher: Tom Smyth
Cover Photos: all images iStock & Shutterstock
Interior Photos: All photos Glyn Genin/APA, except iStock 17, 37, 47, 48, 121, 141, 146, 148, 151,152, 155, 159, 160, 163, 164, 173; Mina Patria 24; Greg Gladman 123; Beverley Speight 145; James Macdonald/APA 177

Distribution

UK, Ireland and Europe
Apa Publications (UK) Ltd
sales@insightguides.com
United States and Canada
Ingram Publisher Services
ips@ingramcontent.com
Australia and New Zealand
Woodslane
info@woodslane.com.au
Southeast Asia
Apa Publications (SN) Pte
singaporeoffice@insightguides.com

Worldwide
Apa Publications (UK) Ltd
sales@insightguides.com

Special Sales, Content Licensing, and CoPublishing
Discounts available for bulk quantities. We can create special editions, personalized jackets, and corporate imprints. sales@insightguides.com; www.insightguides.biz

Contents

Survival

Food & Drink

People

In an Emergency

Dictionary

Pronunciation

This section is designed to make you familiar with the sounds of Norwegian by using our simplified phonetic transcription. You'll find the pronunciation of the Norwegian letters explained below, together with their 'imitated' equivalents (the Norwegian alphabet is the same as in English, with the addition of the letters **æ**, **ø** and **å**). This phonetic system is used throughout the phrase book; simply read the pronunciation as if it were English, noting any special rules below.

Stress has been indicated in the phonetic transcription with underlining, tone with the accent marks and long vowels with bold.

Consonants

Letter	Approximate Pronunciation	Symbol	Example	Pronunciation
g	1. before i and y, (sometimes before ei) like y in yes	**y**	**gi**	*yee*
	2. elsewhere, like g in go	**g**	**gått**	*goht*
gj	like y in yes	**y**	**gjest**	*yehst*
j	like y in yes	**y**	**ja**	*yah*
k	1. before i, y and ei like h in hue, but with the tongue raised a little higher	**kh**	**kino**	*khee´·nu*
	2. elsewhere, like k in kit	**k**	**kaffe**	*kahf´·fuh*
kj	like h in hue, but with the tongue raised a little higher	**kh**	**kjøre**	*khur`·ruh*

Letter	Approximate Pronunciation	Symbol	Example	Pronunciation
r	rolled near the front of the mouth	**r**	**rare**	_rah`•ruh_
s	like s in sit	**s**	**spise**	_spee`•suh_
sj	like sh in shut	**sh**	**stasjon**	_stah•shoo´n_
sk	1. before i and y (sometimes before øy), like sh in shut	**sh**	**ski**	_shee_
	2. elsewhere, like sk in skate	**sk**	**skole**	_skoo`•luh_
skj	like sh in shut	**sh**	**skje**	_sheh_
w	like v in vice	**v**	**whisky**	_vihs´•kih_
z	like s in sit	**s**	**zoom**	_soom_

Letters b, c, d, f, h, l, m, n, p, q, t, v, x are generally pronounced as in English.

Vowels

Letter	Approximate Pronunciation	Symbol	Example	Pronunciation
a	1. like a in father, but longer	**ah**	**tak**	_tahk_
	2. like a in father	**ah**	**takk**	_tahk_
e	1. like e in get, but longer	**eh**	**sent**	_sehnt_
	2. like e in get	**eh**	**penn**	_pehn_
	3. like a in bad	**a**	**her**	_har_
	4. before r, like a in bad	**a**	**herre**	_ha`•ruh_
	5. like u in uncle	**uh**	**sitte**	_sih`•tuh_

Letter	Approximate Pronunciation	Symbol	Example	Pronunciation
i	1. like ee in bee	**ee**	**hit**	*heet*
	2. like i in sit	**ih**	**sitt**	*siht*
o	1. like oo in soon, with lips tightly rounded	**oo**	**ord**	*oor*
	2. like aw in saw	**aw**	**tog**	*tawg*
	3. like u i put, with lips tightly rounded	**u**	**ost**	*ust*
	4. like o in cloth	**oh**	**stoppe**	*stohp`•puh*
	5. before r, like oo in soon	**oo**	**hvor**	*voor*
u	1. like ew in few, but longer	**ew**	**mur**	*mewr*
	2. like ew in few	**ew**	**busk**	*bewsk*
	3. like u in put, with lips tightly rounded	**u**	**bukk**	*buk*
y	1. like ui in fruit, but longer	**ui**	**myr**	*muir*
	2. like ui in fruit	**ui**	**bygge**	*buig`•guh*
æ	1. like a in bad, but longer	**a**	**lære**	*la`•ruh*
	2. like a in bad	**a**	**færre**	*far´•ruh*
ø	1. like ur in fur, but longer and with lips rounded	**ur**	**blø**	*blur*
	2. like ur in fur, with lips rounded	**ur**	**sønn**	*surn*

Letter	Approximate Pronunciation	Symbol	Example	Pronunciation
å	1. like aw in saw, but longer	**aw**	**såpe**	_saw`_•puh
	2. like o in cloth	**oh**	**gått**	goht

Vowel Combinations

Letter	Approximate Pronunciation	Symbol	Example	Pronunciation
ai	like ie in tie	**ie**	**mais**	mies
au	like ev in ever	**ev**	**sau**	sev
ei	like ay in say	**ay**	**geit**	yayt
eg	at the end of a word and before n, like ay in say	**ay**	**jeg**	yay
oi	like oi in oil	**oi**	**koie**	_koi`_•uh
øy	like ur + y	**ury**	**høy**	hury

In Norwegian, vowel length distinguishes meaning. All vowels come in two lengths, long and short. Long vowels are in bold throughout the phonetics.

Norwegian is a tonal language. This means that tone is used to distinguish between certain words, which otherwise would sound the same. For example:

hender (_hehn´_•_nuhr_), tone 1 = plural of **hånd** (hand)
hender (_hehn`_•_nuhr_), tone 2 = present tense of **hende** (happen)

In the phonetics, tone 1, which is a rising tone (i.e., starts low and rises in pitch) is marked with the acute accent (´); tone 2, which is a falling tone (i.e., starts high and lowers in pitch), with the grave accent (`).

In Norwegian, consonants are silent in the following situations:
1. The letter **d** is generally silent after **l**, **n** or **r** (e.g. **holde**, **land**, **gård**), and sometimes at the end of words (e.g. **god**, **med**).
2. The letter **g** is silent in the endings **-lig** and **-ig**.
3. The letter **h** is silent when followed by a consonant (e.g. **hjem**, **hva**).
4. The letter **t** is silent in the definite form ('the') of neuter nouns (e.g., **eplet**) and in the pronoun **det**.
5. The letter **v** is silent in certain words (e.g. **selv**, **tolv**, **halv**).
6. In the eastern part of Norway the letter **r** is silent when followed by **l**, **n**, **s**, **t** (and sometimes **d**). These consonants are pronounced with the tip of the tongue turned up well behind the front teeth. The **r** then ceases to be pronounced, but influences the tone of the following consonant. This 'retroflex' pronunciation also occurs in words ending with an **r** if the following word begins with a **d**, **l**, **n**, **s** or **t**.

How to use this Book

Sometimes you see two alternatives separated by a slash. Choose the one that's right for your situation.

ESSENTIAL

I'm here on vacation [holiday]/business.

Jeg er her på ferie/i forretninger. *yay ar har paw feh´r•yuh/ih fohr•reht´•nihng•uhr*

I'm going to...

Jeg reiser til... *yay rays`•uhr tihl...*

I'm staying at the...Hotel.

Jeg bor på Hotell... *yay boor paw hu•tehl´...*

Words you may see are shown in YOU MAY SEE boxes.

YOU MAY SEE...

BUSSHOLDEPLASS/ TRIKKEHOLDEPLASS bus stop/tram stop

INNGANG/UTGANG enter/exit

STEMPLE BILLETTEN stamp your ticket

Any of the words or phrases listed can be plugged into the sentence below.

Tickets

Where's...?

Hvor er det...? *voor ar deh...*

the ATM

en minibank *ehn mee´•nih•bangk*

the bank

en bank *ehn bahngk*

the currency exchange office

et vekslingskontor *eht vehk`s•lihngs•kun•toor*

Norwegian phrases appear in purple.

Read the simplified pronunciation as if it were English. For more on pronunciation, see page 7.

Personal

Are you married?	**Er du gift?** *ar dew yihft*
I'm...	**Jeg er...** *yay ar...*
single	**singel** *ew`•yift*
in a relationship	**opptatt** *ohp´•taht*
married	**gift** *yift*
I'm widowed.	**Jeg er enkemann m /enke f.** *yay ar ehng`•kuh•mahn/ehng`•kuh*

For Numbers, see page 170.

Related phrases can be found by going to the page number indicated.

When different gender forms apply, the masculine form is followed by *m*; feminine by *f*

Norwegians tend to get right to business and don't engage in much small talk or socializing. You'll find them to be serious and direct in business dealings and in their manner of speaking in general.

Information boxes contain relevant country, culture and language tips.

Expressions you may hear are shown in You May Hear boxes.

YOU MAY HEAR...

Neste! *nehs`•tuh*	Next!
Billetten/Passet, takk. *bil•leht´•tuhn/pahs´•suh tahk*	Your ticket/passport, please.

Color-coded side bars identify each section of the book.

Survival

Arrival & Departure

ESSENTIAL

I'm here on vacation [holiday]/business. **Jeg er her på ferie/i forretninger.** *yay ar har paw feh´r•yuh/ih fohr•reht´•nihng•uhr*

I'm going to... **Jeg reiser til...** *yay rays`•uhr tihl...*

I'm staying at the... Hotel. **Jeg bor på Hotell...** *yay boor paw hu•tehl´...*

YOU MAY HEAR...

Billetten/Passet, takk. *bihl•leht´•tuhn/ pahs´•suh tahk*
Your ticket/passport, please.

Hva er formålet med reisen? *vah ar fohr`•maw•luh meh ray`•suhn*
What's the purpose of your trip?

Hvor skal du bo? *voor skahl dew boo*
Where are you staying?

Hvor lenge blir du? *voor lehng`•uh bleer dew*
How long are you staying?

Hvem reiser du sammen med? *vehm ray`• suhr dew sahm´•muhn meh*
Who are you with?

Border Control

I'm just passing through. **Jeg er bare på gjennomreise.** *yay ar bah´•ruh paw yehn`•nohm•ray•suh*

I would like to declare... **Jeg vil gjerne fortolle...** *yay vihl ya`r•nuh fohr•tohl´•luh...*

I have nothing to declare. **Jeg har ingenting å fortolle.** *yay hahr ihng`•uhn• tihng aw fohr•tohl´•luh*

YOU MAY HEAR...

Har du noe å fortolle? _hahr dew noo`·uh aw fohr·tohl´·luh_ — Do you have anything to declare?

Du må betale toll for dette. _dew maw buh·tah´·luh tohl fohr deht`·tuh_ — You must pay duty on this.

Vær så snill å åpne denne bagen. _var saw snihl aw aw`p·nuh dehn`·nuh behg´·guhn_ — Please open this bag.

Money

ESSENTIAL

Where's...?	**Hvor er det...?** _voor ar deh..._
the ATM	**en minibank** _ehn mee´·nih·bangk_
the bank	**en bank** _ehn bahngk_
the currency exchange office	**et vekslingskontor** _eht vehk`s·lihngs·kun·toor_
What time does the bank open/close?	**Når åpner/stenger banken?** _nohr aw´p·nuhr/ stehng`·uhr bahng´·kuhn_
I'd like to change some dollars/pounds.	**Jeg vil gjerne veksle noen dollar/pund.** _yay vihl ya´r·nuh vehk`s·luh noo`·uhn dohl´·lahr/pewn_
I'd like to cash a traveler's check [cheque].	**Jeg vil gjerne løse inn en reisesjekk.** _yay vihl ya´r· nuh lur`·suh ihn ehn ray`·suh·shehk_

At the Bank

Can I exchange foreign currency here?	**Kan jeg veksle utenlandsk valuta her?** _kahn yay vehk`s·luh ew´·tuhn·lahnsk vah·lew´·tah har_

YOU MAY SEE...

The Norwegian currency is the **krone** (crown), abbreviated to **kr** or **NOK**, divided into 100 **øre**.
Coins: 50 **øre**; **kr** 1, 5, 10 and 20
Notes: **kr** 50, 100, 200, 500 and 1,000

What's the exchange rate?	**Hva er vekslingskursen?** *vah ar vehk`s•lihngs•kewr•suhn*
How much is the fee?	**Hvor mye tar dere i kommisjon?** *voor mui`•uh tahr deh`•ruh ih ku•mih•shoo´n*
I've lost my traveler's checks [cheques].	**Jeg har mistet reisesjekkene.** *yay hahr mihs`•tuht ray`•suh•shehk•kuh•nuh*
My card was lost.	**Jeg har mistet kortet.** *yay hahr mihs`•tuht kohr´•tuh*
My credit cards have been stolen.	**Kredittkortene mine ble stjålet.** *kreh•diht´•kohr•tuh•nuh mee`•nuh bleh styaw`•luht*
My card doesn't work.	**Kortet virker ikke.** *kohr´•tuh vihr`•kuhr ihk`•kuh*
The ATM ate my card.	**Minibanken spiste kortet mitt.** *mee•nih•bangk•en spih•ste kurt•e miht*

Cash can be obtained from **minibank** (ATMs), which can be readily found in urban areas . Most major credit cards and some debit cards are accepted. You will need a PIN that is compatible with European machines, usually a four-digit, numeric code. ATMs offer good rates, though there may be hidden fees.

Vekslingskontor (currency exchange offices), banks and post offices are options for exchanging currency. Exchange offices are found at airports, train stations, ship terminals and in many tourist centers. Banks are generally open Monday to Friday 8:15 a.m. to 3:30 p.m., though some close later one day a week and hours may vary in the provinces. Remember to bring your passport, in case you are asked for identification.

ESSENTIAL

How do I get to town?	**Hvordan kommer jeg til byen?** <u>voor</u>´•dahn <u>kohm</u>´•muhr yay tihl <u>bui</u>´•uhn
Where is…?	**Hvor er…?** voor ar…
the airport	**flyplassen** <u>flui</u>´•plahs•suhn
the train station	**jernbanestasjonen** <u>ya</u>`n•bah•nuh•stah•sho͞on•uhn
the bus station	**busstasjonen** bews´•stah•sho͞on•uhn
the subway [underground] station	**T-banestasjonen** <u>teh</u>´•bah•nuh•stah•sho͞on•uhn
How far is it?	**Hvor langt er det?** voor <u>lahngt</u> <u>ar</u> deh
Where can I buy tickets?	**Hvor kan jeg kjøpe billetter?** voor kahn yay <u>khur</u>`•puh bihl•<u>leht</u>´•tuhr
A one-way [single]/ round-trip [return] ticket.	**En enveisbillett/tur-returbillett.** ehn <u>ehn</u>´•vays•bihl•leht/tewr•reh•<u>tew</u>´r•bil•leht
How much?	**Hvor mye koster det?** voor <u>mui</u>`•uh kohs`•tuhr deh
Are there any discounts?	**Er det noen rabatter?** <u>ar</u> deh <u>noo</u>`•uhn rah•<u>baht</u>´•tuhr
Which…?	**Hvilken…?** <u>vihl</u>´•kuhn…
gate	**utgang** <u>ew</u>`t•gahng
line	**linje** <u>lihn</u>`•yuh
platform	**perrong** pehr•<u>rohng</u>´
Where can I get a taxi?	**Hvor kan jeg få tak i en drosje?** voor kahn yay faw tahk ih ehn <u>drohsh</u>`•uh
Can you take me to this address?	**Kan du kjøre meg til denne adressen?** kahn dew <u>khur</u>`•ruh may tihl <u>dehn</u>`•nuh ahd•<u>rehs</u>´•suhn
Where can I rent a car?	**Hvor kan jeg leie bil?** voor kahn yay <u>lay</u>`•uh b<u>ee</u>l
Can I have a map?	**Kan jeg få et kart?** kahn yay faw eht kahrt

Tickets

When's…to Stavanger?	**Når går…til Stavanger?** *nohr gawr…tihl stah•vahng´•uhr*
the (first) bus	**(første) buss** *(furrs`•tuh) bews*
the (next) flight	**(neste) fly** *(nehs`•tuh) flui*
the (last) train	**(siste) tog** *(sihs`•tuh) tawg*
Where can I buy tickets?	**Hvor kan jeg kjøpe billetter?** *voor kahn yay khur`•puh bihl•leht´•tuhr*
One ticket/ please.	**En billett/To billetter, takk.** *ehn bihl•leht´/too bihl•leht´•tuhr tak*
For today/tomorrow.	**For i dag/i morgen.** *fohr ih•dahg/ih•mawr`•uhn*
A one-way [single]/ round-trip [return] ticket.	**En enveisbillett/tur-returbillett.** *ehn ehn´•vays•bihl•leht/tewr•reh•tew´r•bil•leht*
A first class/economy class ticket.	**En billett på første klasse/ turistklasse.** *ehn bihl•eht´ poh furrs`•tuh klahs`•suh/tew•rihst´•klahs•suh*
How much?	**Hvor mye koster det?** *voor mui`•uh kohs`•tuhr deh*
Is there a discount for…?	**Er det noen rabatt for…?** *ar deh noo`•uhn rah•baht´ fohr…*
children	**barn** *bahrn*
students	**studenter** *stew•dehn´•tuhr*
senior citizens	**pensjonister** *pahng•shoo•nihs´•tuhr*
The express bus/ express train, please.	**Ekspressbuss/ekspresstog, er du snill** *eks•pruhs•bews/eks•pruhs•tawg, ar dew snihl*
The local bus/train, please.	**Lokalbuss/-tog, er du snill** *loh•kahl•bews/tawg, ar dew snihl*
I have an e-ticket.	**Jeg har en e-billett.** *yay hahr ehn eh´•bihl•leht*
Can I buy a ticket on the bus/train?	**Kan man kjøpe billett på bussen/toget?** *kahn mahn khur`•puh bihl•leht´ poh bews`•suhn/taw´•guh*
Do I have to stamp the ticket before boarding?	**Må jeg stemple billetten før jeg går ombord?** *maw yay stam•pleh bill•eht•ehn fur yay gawr awm•bohr*

YOU MAY HEAR...

Hvilket selskap flyr du med? *vihl`·kuht sehl`·skahp fluir dew meh* — What airline are you flying?

Innenlands eller utenlands? *ihn`·nuhn·lahns ehl`·luhr ew`·tuhn·lahns* — Domestic or international?

Hvilken terminal? *vihl`·kuhn tehr·mih·nahl`* — What terminal?

How long is this ticket valid? **Hvor lenge er denne billetten gyldig?** *voor lehn·geh ar dehn·neh beel·eht·ehn yil·deeg*

Can I return on the same ticket? **Er det tur/retur?** *ar deh tewr/reh·tewr*

I'd like to...my reservation. **Jeg vil gjerne...reservasjonen.** *yay vihl ya`r·nuh...reh·sehr·vah·shoo´n·uhn*

cancel **annullere** *ahn·newl·leh´·ruh*

change **endre** *ehn`·druh*

confirm **bekrefte** *buh·krehf´·tuh*

For Days, see page 172.

For Time, see page 171.

Plane

Airport Transfer

How much is a taxi to the airport? **Hva koster drosje til flyplassen?** *vah kohs`·tuhr drohsh`·uh tihl flui´·plahs·suhn*

To...Airport, please. **Til...lufthavn.** *tihl...lewft´·hahvn*

My airline is... **Jeg flyr med...** *yay fluir meh...*

My flight leaves at... **Flyet mitt går...** *flui´·uh miht gawr...*

I'm in a hurry. **Jeg har dårlig tid.** *yay hahr dawr`·lih teed*

Can you take an alternate route?	**Kan du kjøre en annen vei?** *kahn dew khur`•ruh ehn ahn`•nuhn vay*
Can you drive faster/ slower?	**Kan du kjøre fortere/saktere?** *kahn dew khur`•ruh foor`•tuh•ruh/sahk`•tuh•ruhw*

YOU MAY SEE...

ANKOMST	arrivals
AVGANG	departures
BAGASJEBÅND	baggage claim
SIKKERHETSVAKT	security
INNENLAND	domestic flights
UTLAND	international flights
INNSJEKKING	check-in
INNSJEKKING MED E-BILLETT	e-ticket check-in
GATE FOR AVGANG	departure gates

YOU MAY HEAR...

Neste! _nehs`·tuh_

Billetten/Passet, takk. _bil·leht´·tuhn/_
pahs´·suh tahk

Hvor mange kolli har du? _voor mang`·uh_
kohl´·lih hahr dew

Du har for mye bagasje. _dew hahr fohr_
mui´·uh bah·gah´·shuh

Den er for tung/stor til håndbagasje. _dehn_
ar fohr tung/stoor tihl hohn`·bah·gah´·shuh

Har du pakket disse veskene/ koffertene
selv? _hahr dew pahk´·kuht dihs`·suh_
vehs´·kuh·nuh/kuf´·fuhr·tuh·nuh sehl

Tar du med noe for andre? _tahr dew meh_
noo`·uh fohr ahn`·druh

Tøm lommene. _turm lum`·muh·nuh_

Ta av deg skoene. _tah ah day skoo´·uh·nuh_

Avgang...er nå klar for ombordstigning.
ahv`·gahng...ar naw klahr fohr
ohm·boor´·steeg·nihng

Next!

Your ticket/passport,
please.

How many pieces of
luggage do you have?

You have excess luggage.

That's too heavy/large for
a carry-on [to carry on
board].

Did you pack these bags/
suitcases yourself?

Did anyone give you
anything to carry?

Empty your pockets.

Take off your shoes.

Now boarding flight...

Checking In

Where's check-in?	**Hvor er innsjekkingsskranken?** _voor ar_ _ihn´·shehk·kihngs·skrahng·kuhn_
My name is...	**Jeg heter...** _yay heh`·tuhr..._
I'm going to...	**Jeg skal til...** _yay skahl tihl..._
I have...	**Jeg har...** _yay hahr_
one suitcase	**en koffert** _ehn kohf·uhrt_

two suitcases	**to kofferter**	*toh kohf•uhrt•uhr*
one piece of hand luggage	**en håndbagasje**	*ehn hawn•bahg•ahsh•uh*
How much luggage is allowed?	**Hvor mye bagasje har man lov å ha med?**	*voor mui`•uh bah•gah´•shuh hahr mahn lawv oh hah meh*
Is that pounds or kilos?	**Er det i pund eller kilo?**	*ar deht•uh ee pewn ehl•uhr shee•loh*
Which terminal?	**Hvilken terminal?**	*vee´k•uhn tar•mihn•ahl*
Which gate?	**Hvilken gate?**	*vee´k•uhn gayt*
Can I have a window/ an aisle seat?	**Kan jeg få plass ved vinduet/midtgangen?**	*kahn yay faw plahs veh vihn`•dew•uh/miht`•gahng•uhn*
When do we leave/ arrive?	**Når drar vi/kommer vi fram?**	*nohr drahr vee/kohm´•muhr vee frahm*
Is the flight delayed?	**Er flyet forsinket?**	*ar flui´•uh fohr•sihng´•kuht*
How late will it be?	**Hvor sent vil det bli?**	*voor sehnt vihl deh blee*

Luggage

Where is/are…?	**Hvor er…?**	*voor ar…*
the luggage carts [trolleys]	**bagasjetrallene**	*bah•gah´•shuh•trahl•luh•nuh*
the luggage lockers	**oppbevaringsboksene**	*ohp´•buh•vah´•rihngs•bohk•su h•nuh*

the baggage claim	**bagasjeutleveringen**
	bah•gah´•shuh•ewt•leh•veh•ri hng•uhn
My luggage has been lost/stolen.	**Bagasjen min er tapt/stjålet.**
	bahg•ahsh•uhn mihn ar tahpt/stjawl•uht
My suitcase was damaged.	**Kofferten min ble skadet.**
	kuf´•fuhr•tuhn mihn bleh skah`•duht

Finding your Way

Where is...?	**Hvor er...?** *voor ar...*
the currency exchange office	**vekslingskontoret** *vehks`•lihngs•kun•too•ruh*
the exit	**utgangen** *ewt`•gahng•uhn*
the taxi stand [rank]	**drosjeholdeplassen** *drohsh`•uh•hol•luh•plahs•suhn*
the car hire	**bilutleie** *beel•ewt•lay•eh*
Is there... into town?	**Går det... inn til byen?** *gawr deh... ihn tihl by•ehn*
a bus	**en buss** *ehn bews*
a train	**et tog** *eht tawg*
an underground station	**En T-bane** *ehn teh•bahn•eh*

For Asking Directions, see page 34.

YOU MAY HEAR...

Ta plass. *tah plahs*	All aboard.
Billetter, takk. *bihl•leht´•tuhr tahk*	Tickets, please.
Du må bytte i... *dew maw buit`•tuh ih...*	You have to change at...
Neste holdeplass... *nehs`•tuh hohl`•luh•plahs...*	Next stop...

Norway runs a train network more than 4,000 km (c. 2,500 miles) long, though the system is much more comprehensive in the south than the north. Oslo is the main hub for most long-distance, express and local trains. Long-distance lines that span the country are an excellent way to view the incredible Norwegian scenery. A number of discounts are available: children under 4 travel free of charge, and children under 16 and senior citizens travel at half price. Local buses, trams, subways and ferries run on an integrated network, so you may transfer at no additional cost. Keep in mind that buying a **flexikort** (multi-trip ticket) is cheaper than buying single tickets. For moving around the capital, you may also want to consider a 1-, 2- or 3-day (children's or family) **Oslo Pass**, which offers unlimited public transportation within greater Oslo and free entry to a number of museums and tourist attractions. For long-distance travel, passes such as Eurorail (non-European residents), InterRail (European residents) or ScanRail (for travel within Scandinavia) can offer better value fares.

Train

How do I get to the train station?	**Hvordan kommer jeg til jernbanestasjonen?** _voor´•dahn kohm´•muhr yay tihl ya´rn•bah•nuh•stah•shoo•nuhn_
Is it far from here?	**Er det langt herfra?** _ar deh lahngt ha´r•frah_
Where is/are...?	**Hvor er...?** _voor ar..._
the ticket office	**billettluken** _bihl•leht´•lew•kuhn_
the information desk	**informasjonsskranken** _ihn•fohr•mah•shoo´ns•skrahng•kuhn_
the platforms	**perrongene** _par•awng•ehn•uh_
the luggage lockers	**bagasjeskapene** _bahg•ahsh•uh•skahp•ehn•uh_
Can I have a train schedule [timetable]?	**Kan jeg få en togtabell?** _kahn yay faw ehn tawg´•tah•behl_
How long is the trip?	**Hvor lang er turen?** _voor lang ar tew´•ruhn_
Is it a direct train?	**Går toget direkte?** _gawr tawg•eht deeh•rehk•teh_
Do I have to change trains?	**Må jeg bytte tog?** _maw yay buit`•tuh taw_
Is the train on time?	**Er toget i rute?** _ar tawg•eht ee rewt•eh_

For Tickets, see page 20.

Departures

Which track [platform] does the train to Skien leave from?	**Fra hvilket spor går toget til Skien?** _frah vihl´•kuht spoor gawr taw´•guh til sheh´•uhn_
Is this the track [platform] to...?	**Er dette sporet til...?** _ar deht`•tuh spoo´•ruh tihl..._
Where is track [platform]...?	**Hvor er spor...?** _voor ar spoor..._
Where do I change for...?	**Hvor må jeg bytte for å komme til...?** _voor maw yay buit`•tuh fohr aw kohm`•muh tihl..._

On Board

Is this seat taken?	**Er denne plassen opptatt?** _ar dehn`•nuh plahs´•suhn ohp´•taht_
Can I sit here?	**Kan jeg sitte her?** _kahn yay siht•uh har_
Can I open the window?	**Kan jeg åpne vinduet?** _kahn yay awpn•eh vihn•dew•eh_
I think that's my seat.	**Jeg tror at det er min plass.** _yay troor aht deh ar meen plahs_
Here's my reservation.	**Her er reservasjonen min.** _har ar rehs•ehr•vahsh•un•uhn mihn_

Bus

Where's the bus station?	**Hvor er busstasjonen?** _voor ar bews´•sta•shoo•nuhn_
How far is it?	**Hvor langt er det?** _voor lahngt ar deh_
How do I get to…?	**Hvordan kommer jeg til…?** _voor´•dahn kohm´•muhr yay tihl…_
Does the bus/train stop at (place/area)…?	**Stopper bussen/trikken (ved/på)…?** _stohp`•puhr bews´•suhn/trihk´•kuhn (veh/poh)…_
Can you tell me when to get off?	**Kan du si meg når jeg skal av?** _kahn dew see may nohr yay skahl ah_
Do I have to change buses?	**Må jeg bytte buss?** _maw yay buit`•tuh bews_

YOU MAY SEE…

BUSSHOLDEPLASS/ TRIKKEHOLDEPLASS	bus stop/train stop
STOPP	request stop
INNGANG/UTGANG	enter/exit
STEMPLE BILLETTEN	stamp your ticket

| Can you stop here? | **Kan du stoppe her?** *kahn dew <u>stohp`</u>•puh har* |

For Asking Directions, see page 34.

T-bane

Where's the nearest subway [underground] station?	**Hvor er nærmeste T-banestasjon?** *voor ar <u>nar`</u>•mehs•tuh <u>teh´</u>•bah•nuh•stah•shoon*
Can I have a map of the subway [underground]?	**Kan jeg få et kart over T-banen?** *kahn yay faw eht kart <u>aw´</u>•vuhr <u>teh´</u>•bah•nuh*
Which line for...?	**Hvilken linje går til...?** *<u>vihl´</u>•kuhn <u>lihn`</u>•yuh gawr tihl...*
Which direction?	**Hvilken retning?** *vee´k•ehn reht•nihng*
Where do I change for...?	**Hvor må jeg bytte for å komme til...?** *voor maw yay <u>buit`</u>•tuh fohr aw <u>kohm`</u>•muh tihl...*
Is this the right train for...?	**Er dette toget til... ?** *ar <u>deht`</u>•tuh <u>taw´</u>•guh tihl...*
How many stops to...	**Hvor mange stoppesteder er det før...?** *voor mahn•geh stohp•puh•steh•duhr ar deh fur*
Where are we?	**Hvor er vi?** *voor ar vee*

For Tickets, see page 20.

The Oslo **Tunnelbane** or **T-bane** (subway) runs from approximately 5:30 a.m. to just after midnight. Buying a **flexikort** (multi-trip ticket) is a good idea if you plan on making numerous trips. It can be used to make transfers within one hour at no extra charge. An **Oslo Pass** is another discount travel pass, good for all forms of public transportation.

Boat & Ferry

When does the boat/ ferry for…leave?	**Når går båten/fergen til…?**	*nohr gawr b<u>aw</u>´•tuhn/ f<u>ehr</u>´•guhn tihl…*
Can I take my car?	**Kan jeg ta med bilen?**	*kahn yay t<u>ah</u>`•meh b<u>ee</u>´•luhn*
What time is the next sailing?	**Når er neste avgang?**	*nawr ar nehs•tuh ahv•gahng*
Can I book a seat/cabin?	**Kan jeg bestille en plass/lugar?**	*kahn yay behs•tihl•uh ehn plahs/lewg•ahr*
How long is the crossing?	**Hvor lang er overfarten?**	*voor lahng ar awv•ehr•fahrt•ehn*

For Tickets, see page 20.

Ferry and boat travel is efficient in Norway. Most ferries and high-speed ships have frequent departure schedules, so you rarely have to wait in lines, and the cost for passenger and car transport is generally low. Besides regular ferry service, several companies offer cruises along the fjords. These are very popular during the summer months and tickets are more expensive during this period, so reservations should be made well in advance.

Taxi

Where can I get a taxi?	**Hvor kan jeg få tak i en drosje?**	*voor kahn yay f<u>aw</u> t<u>ah</u>k ih ehn <u>droh</u>`•shuh*
I'd like a taxi now/ for tomorrow at…	**Jeg trenger en drosje nå/i morgen klokken…**	*yay tr<u>ehng</u>´•uhr ehn <u>droh</u>`•shuh n<u>aw</u>/ih m<u>awr</u>`•uhn <u>klohk</u>`•kuhn…*
Can you pick me up…?	**Kan du hente meg…?**	*kahn dew <u>hehn</u>`•tuh may…*
at the airport	**på flyplassen**	*poh flu<u>i</u>´•plahs•suhn*
at the ferry landing	**ved fergeleiet**	*veh fer`•guh•lay•uh*
at eight o'clock	**klokken åtte**	*<u>klohk</u>`•kuhn oht`•tuh*

Take me to…	**Kjør meg til…** *khurr may tihl…*
this address	**denne adressen** <u>*dehn*</u>`*·nuh ahd·*<u>*rehs*</u>´*·suhn*
the airport	**flyplassen** <u>*flui*</u>´*·plahs·suhn*
the train station	**jernbanestasjonen** <u>*ya*</u>`*rn·bah·nuh·stah·shoon·uhn*
I'm in a hurry.	**Jeg har dårlig tid.** *yay* <u>*hahr*</u> *dawr*`*·lih* *teed*
Can you drive faster/ slower?	**Kan du kjøre fortere/saktere?** *kahn dew* <u>*khur*</u>`*·ruh* <u>*fohr*</u>`*·tuh·ruh/*<u>*sahk*</u>`*·tuh·ruh*

Taxis can be hailed in the street, found at taxi stands or ordered by phone. All cabs are metered and service charges are included in the fare. You can tip the driver by rounding up the fare. Keep in mind that rates differ from place to place and travel by taxi is generally expensive, so ask for an approximate fare beforehand. Most taxis accept credit cards but be sure to double check first.

YOU MAY HEAR…

Hvor skal du? *voor* <u>*skahl*</u> *dew*	Where to?
Hva var adressen? *vah vahr ahd·*<u>*rehs*</u>´*·suhn*	What's the address?

Stop/Wait here.	**Stopp/Vent her.** *stohp/vehnt har*
How much?	**Hvor mye koster det?** *voor mui`·uh kohs`·tuhr deh*
You said…crowns.	**Du sa…kroner.** *dew sah…kroo`·nuhr*
Can I have a receipt?	**Kan jeg få en kvittering?** *kahn yay faw ehn kviht·teh´·rihng*
Keep the change.	**Behold vekslepengene.** *buh·hohl´ vehk`s·luh·pehng·uh·nuh*

Bicycle & Motorbike

I'd like to rent [hire]…	**Jeg vil gjerne leie…** *yay vihl ya`r·nuh lay`·uh…*
a bicycle	**en sykkel** *ehn suik´·kuhl*
a moped	**en moped** *ehn mu·peh´d*
a motorcycle	**en motorsykkel** *ehn moo´·toor·suik·kuhl*
How much per day/week?	**Hvor mye koster det per dag/uke?** *voor mui`·uh kohs`·tuhr deh pehr dahg/ew`·kuh*
Can I have a helmet/lock?	**Kan jeg få med hjelm/lås?** *kahn yay faw`·meh yehlm/laws*

If you enjoy cycling there are many well-planned routes throughout the country, through lush valleys and breathtaking fjords. Attractions are usually signposted. You can bring your own bike or rent one easily. Given the terrain, a **terrengsykkel** (mountain bike) is usually the most practical option.

Car Hire

Where can I rent a car?	**Hvor kan jeg leie en bil?** *voor kahn yay lay`·uh ehn beel*
I'd like to rent [hire]…	**Jeg vil gjerne leie…** *yay vihl ya`r·nuh lay`·uh…*
a 2-/4-door car	**en to-dørs/firedørs bil** *ehn too´·durrs/fee`·ruh·durrs beel*

an automatic	**en bil med automatgir** *meh ev·tu·mah´t·geer*
a car with air conditioning	**en bil med klimaanlegg** *ehn beel meh klee´·mah·ahn·lehg*
a car seat	**et barnesete** *eht bahr´·nuh·seh·tuh*
a cheap/small car	**en billig/liten bil** *ehn bihl·ih/liht·ehn beel*

YOU MAY HEAR...

Har du et internasjonalt førerkort? *hahr dew eht ihn´·tuhr·nah·shu·nahlt fur´·ruhr·kohrt*	Do you have an international driver's license?
Kan jeg få se passet? *kahn yay faw seh pahs´·suh*	Can I see your passport?
Vil du ha forsikring? *vihl dew hah fohr·sihk´·rihng*	Do you want insurance?
Det er et depositum på... *deh ar eht deh·poo´·sih·tewm poh...*	There is a deposit of...
Undertegn her. *ewn`·nuhr·tayn har*	Please sign here.

How much...?	**Hvor mye koster det...?** *voor mui`·uh kohs`·tuhr deh...*
per day	**per dag** *pehr dahg*
per week	**per uke** *pehr ew`·kuh*
per kilometer	**per kilometer** *pehr khee´·lu·meh·tuhr*
for unlimited mileage	**for ubegrenset kjørelengde** *fohr ew`·buh·grehn·suht khur`·ruh·lehng·duh*
with insurance	**inkludert forsikring** *ihn·klew·dehrt´ fohr·sihk´·rihng*
Are there any discounts?	**Er det noen rabatter?** *ar deh noo`·uhn rah·baht´·tuhr*

Fuel Station

Where's the nearest gas [petrol] station?	**Hvor er nærmeste bensinstasjon?** *voor ar ner`·mehs·tuh behn·seen´·stah·shoon*
Fill it up, please.	**Full tank, takk.** *fewl tahngk tahk*
...liters, please.	**...liter bensin, takk.** *...lee´·tuhr behn·seen´ tahk*
Can I pay in cash/by credit card?	**Kan jeg betale kontant/med kredittkort?** *kahn yay buh·tah´·luh kun·tahn´t /meh kreh·diht´·kohrt*

YOU MAY SEE...

NORMAL 95 OKTAN	regular
SUPER 98 OKTAN	premium [super]
DIESEL	diesel

Asking Directions

Are we on the right road for...?	**Er dette veien til...?** *ar deht`·tuh vay´·uhn tihl...*
How far is it to...?	**Hvor langt er det til...?** *voor lahngt ar deh tihl...*
Where's...?	**Hvor er...?** *voor ar...*
...Street	**...gate** *...gah`·tuh*
this address	**denne adressen** *dehn`·nuh ahd·rehs´·suhn*

YOU MAY HEAR...

rett frem *reht frehm*	straight ahead
på venstre side *poh vehn´·struh see`·duh*	on the left
på høyre side *poh hury´·ruh see`·duh*	on the right
på/rundt hjørnet *poh/rewnt yurr`·nuh*	on/around the corner
midt imot... *miht ih·moot´...*	opposite...
bak... *bahk...*	behind...
ved siden av... *veh see`·duhn ah...*	next to...
etter... *eht`·tuhr...*	after...
nord/sør *noor/surr*	north/south
øst/vest *urst/vehst*	east/west
ved lyskrysset *veh lui`s·kruis·suh*	at the traffic light
ved veikrysset *veh vay`·kruis·suh*	at the intersection

the highway [motorway]	**motorveien** *moo´·toor·vay·uhn*
Can you show me where I am on the map?	**Kan du vise meg på kartet hvor jeg er?** *kahn dew vee`·suh may paw kahr´·tuh voor yay ar*
I'm lost.	**Jeg har gått meg vill.** *yay hahr goht may vihl*

Parking

Can I park here?	**Kan jeg parkere her?** *kahn yay pahr·keh´·ruh har*
Is there a parking lot [car park] nearby?	**Fins det en parkeringsplass i nærheten?** *fins deh ehn pahr·keh´·rihngs·plahs ih nar´·heh·tuhn*
How much...?	**Hvor mye koster det...?** *voor mui`·uh kohs`·tuhr deh...*
per hour	**per time** *pehr tee`·muh*
per day	**per dag** *pehr dahg*
for overnight	**over natten** *aw`·vuhr naht´·tuhn*

Parking in Norway is restricted, particularly on weekdays. The most common system is the **P-automat** (automated parking meter) when you park your car, then pay for an amount of time at the meter; the meter then prints a ticket to be displayed on your dashboard. Another option is a **P-hus** (parking garage) when you receive a ticket upon entering the garage. Before getting into your car to leave the garage, you must pay for your ticket at an automated machine or a manned booth.

YOU MAY SEE...

	STOPP	stop
	VIKEPLIKT	yield
	PARKERING FORBUDT	no parking
	ÉNVEISKJØRING	one way
	INNKJØRING FORBUDT	no entry
	FORBIKJØRING FORBUDT	no passing
	U-SVING FORBUDT	no U-turn
	GANGFELT	pedestrian crossing

Breakdown & Repair

My car broke down/ won't start. **Bilen har fått motorstopp/starter ikke.** *bee´·luhn hahr foht moo´·toor·stohp/ stahr`·tuhr ihk`·kuh*

Can you fix it (today)? **Kan du reparere den i dag?** *kahn dew reh·pah·reh´·ruh dehn ee dahg*

When will it be ready? **Når er den klar?** *nohr ar dehn klahr*

How much? **Hvor mye koster det?** *voor mui`·uh kohs`·tuhr deh*

I have a puncture/ flat tyre **Jeg har punktert/et flatt dekk** *yay hahr punk·tehrt/ eht flaht dehk*

Accidents

There's been an accident. **Det har skjedd en ulykke.** *deh hahr shehd ehn ew`·lui·kuh*

Call a doctor/an ambulance! **Ring etter lege/sykebil!** *rihng eht`·tuhr leh`·guh/ sui`·kuh·beel*

Places to Stay

ESSENTIAL

Can you recommend a hotel?	**Kan du anbefale et hotell?** *kahn dew ahn´•buh•fah•luh eht hu•tehl´*
I have a reservation.	**Jeg har bestilt rom.** *yay hahr buh•stihlt´ rum*
My name is…	**Jeg heter…** *yay heh´•tuhr…*
Do you have a room…?	**Har dere et rom…?** *hahr deh`•ruh eht rum…*
for one/two	**for én/to** *fohr ehn/too*
with a bathroom	**med bad** *meh bahd*
with air conditioning	**med klimaanlegg** *meh klee´•mah•ahn•lehg*
For tonight.	**For i natt.** *fohr ih naht*
For two nights.	**For to netter.** *fohr too neht´•tuhr*
For one week.	**For en uke.** *fohr ehn ew´•kuh*
How much?	**Hvor mye koster det?** *voor mui`•uh kohs`•tuhr deh*
Do you have anything cheaper?	**Har dere noe rimeligere?** *hahr deh`•ruh noo´•uh ree`•muh•lih•uh•ruh*
When's check-out?	**Når må jeg sjekke ut?** *nohr maw yay shehk`•kuh ewt*
Can I leave this in the safe?	**Kan jeg legge denne/dette igjen i safen?** *kahn yay lehg`•guh dehn`•nuh/deht`•tuh ih•yehn´ ih sayf´•uhn*
Can I leave my bags?	**Kan jeg sette igjen bagasjen?** *kahn yay seht`•tuh ih•yehn´ bah•gah´•shuhn*
Can I have the bill/ a receipt?	**Kan jeg få regningen/en kvittering?** *kahn yay faw ray`•ning•uhn/ehn kviht•teh´•rihng*
I'll pay in cash/by credit card.	**Jeg betaler kontant/med kredittkort.** *yay buh•tah´•luhr kun•tahnt´/meh kreh•diht´•kohrt*

In Norway, there are a variety of accommodation alternatives in addition to more conventional options such as hotels, bed and breakfasts or **husrom** (rooms in private houses) and **vandrerhjem** (hostels). For a unique holiday experience you could consider a **bondegårdsferie** (farm stay), which lets you taste Norwegian farm life firsthand. Similarly, along the coast, you could arrange to stay in **rorbuer** (fisherman's cabins). **Hytter** (chalets or cabins) are available throughout the country as well.

Somewhere to Stay

Can you recommend...?	**Kan du anbefale...?**	kahn d*ew ahn´*·buh·*fah*·luh
a bed and breakfast	**et rom inklusive frokost?**	eht rum ihnk·lews·ihv·eh fru·kawst
a campsite	**en campingplass?**	ehn kamp·ihng·plahs
a hostel	**et hospits?**	eht hus·pihts
a hotel	**et hotel**	eht hu·tehl´
What is it near?	**Hva er det i nærheten?**	vah *a*r deh ih *nar´*·heh·tuhn
How do I get there?	**Hvordan kommer jeg dit?**	*voor´*·dahn *kohm´*·muhr yay d*ee*t

If you didn't reserve a room before your arrival, the local tourist office can provide information and help you to arrange a reservation. The official website of the Norwegian Tourist Board, Visit Norway (www.visitnorway.com), can provide information about locations in particular cities.

At the Hotel

I have a reservation.	**Jeg har bestilt rom.**	*yay hahr buh•stihlt´ rum*
My name is...	**Jeg heter...**	*yay heh`•tuhr...*
Do you have a room...?	**Har dere et rom...?**	*hahr deh`•ruh eht rum...*
with a bathroom/shower	**med bad/dusj**	*meh bahd/dewsh*
with a private toilet	**med toalett**	*meh tu•ah•leht*
with air conditioning	**med klimaanlegg**	*meh klee´•mah•ahn•lehg*
that's smoking/non-smoking	**for røykere/ikke-røykere**	*fohr ruryk`•uh•ruh/ihk`•kuh•ruryk•uhr•uh*
For...	**For...**	*fawr*
tonight	**i natt**	*ee naht*
two nights	**to netter**	*tu neht•ehr*
a week	**en uke**	*ehn ewk•eh*
Can I access the internet?	**Kan jeg bruke internett?**	*kahn yay brew`•kuh ihn´•tuhr•neht*
Does the hotel have...?	**Har hotellet...?**	*hahr hu•tehl´•uh...*
a computer	**en datamaskin**	*ehn dah´•tah•mah•sheen*

Norwegian electricity is generally 220 volts and round two-pin plugs are typically used. British and American appliances may need an adapter.

(wireless) internet service	**(trådløst) Internett**	trawd•lurst ihnt•ar•neht
an elevator [lift]	**heis**	hays
room service	**romservice**	rum`•sur•vihs
a gym	**trimrom**	trihm´•rum
a pool	**et basseng**	eht bahs•ehng
I need...	**Jeg trenger...**	yay trehng´•uhr...
an extra bed	**en ekstra seng**	ehn ehks´•trah sehng
a cot [camp bed]	**en feltseng**	ehn fehlt´•sehng
a crib [child's cot]	**en barneseng**	ehn bahr`•nuh•sehng

YOU MAY SEE...

SKYV/TREKK	push/pull
TOALETT	restroom [toilet]
DUSJ	shower
HEIS	elevator [lift]
TRAPP	stairs
VAREAUTOMATER	vending machines
IS	ice
VASKERI	laundry
IKKE FORSTYRR	do not disturb
BRANNDØR	fire door
NØDUTGANG	emergency/fire exit
VEKKING	wake-up call

Price

How much per night/ week?	**Hvor mye koster det per natt/uke?** *voor mui`·uh kohs`·tuhr deh pehr naht/ew`·kuh*
Does the price include breakfast/sales tax [VAT]?	**Er frokost/moms inkludert i prisen?** *ar froo´·kust/ mums ihn·klu·dehrt´ ih pree´·suhn*
Are there any discounts?	**Har dere noen rabatter?** *hahr dehr·eh nu·ehn rah·baht·ehr*

Preferences

Can I see the room?	**Kan jeg få se rommet?** *kahn yay faw seh paw rum·eht*
I'd like a...room.	**Jeg vil gjerne ha et...rom.** *yay vihl yar·neh hah eht rum*
better	**bedre** *beh·dreh*
bigger	**større** *stur·reh*
cheaper	**billigere** *bihl·ihg·ehr·eh*
quieter	**roligere** *ru·lihg·ehr·eh*
I'll take it.	**Jeg tar det.** *yay tahr deh*
No, I won't take it.	**Nei, jeg vil ikke ha det.** *nai, yay vihl ihk·eh hah deh*

Questions

Where's...?	**Hvor er...?** *voor ar...*
the bar	**baren** *bah´·ruhn*
the bathroom	**toalettet** *tu·ah·leht´·uh*
the elevator [lift]	**heisen** *hay´·suhn*
Can I have...?	**Kan jeg få...?** *kahn yay faw...*
a blanket	**et ullteppe** *eht ewl`·tehp·puh*
an iron	**et strykejern** *eht strui`·kuh·yarn*
a pillow	**en pute** *ehn pew`·tuh*
the room key/ key card	**romnøkkelen/nøkkelkortet?** *rum·nurk·ehl·ehn/ nurk·ehl·kurt·eht*

a soap	**en såpe** ehn <u>saw</u>`·puh
toilet paper	**toalettpapir** tu·ah·<u>leht</u>´·pah·peer
a towel	**et håndkle** eht <u>hohng</u>`·kleh
Do you have an adapter for this?	**Har du en adapter til denne/dette?** <u>hah</u>r dew ehn ahd·<u>ahp</u>´·tuhr tihl <u>dehn</u>`·nuh/<u>deht</u>`·tuh
How do I turn on the lights?	**Hvordan slår jeg på lyset?** <u>voor</u>´·dahn slawr yay poh <u>lui</u>´s·uh
Can you wake me at…?	**Kan du vekke meg klokken…?** kahn dew <u>vehk</u>`·kuh may <u>klohk</u>`·kuhn…
Can I leave this in the safe?	**Kan jeg få legge denne i safen?** kahn yay faw <u>lehg</u>·eh dehn·eh ee sayf·ehn
Could I have my things from the safe?	**Kan jeg få sakene mine fra safen?** kahn yay faw <u>sah</u>`·kuh·nuh <u>mee</u>`·nuh frah <u>say</u>´·fuhn
Is/are there any mail/messages for me?	**Har det kommet noe post/noen beskjed til meg?** hahr deh <u>kohm</u>`·muht <u>noo</u>`·uh pohst/<u>noo</u>`·uhn buh·sh<u>eh</u>´ tihl may
Do you have a laundry service?	**Har dere vaskeritjenester?** hahr dehr·uh vahsk·ehr·ee·tjehn·ehst·uhr

---

YOU MAY HEAR…

Passet/kredittkortet ditt, takk. <u>pah</u>´·suh/kreh·<u>diht</u>´·kohr·tuh diht tahk — Your passport/credit card, please.

Kan du fylle ut dette skjemaet? kahn dew <u>fui</u>`·luh **ew**t <u>deht</u>´·tuh sh<u>eh</u>`·mah·uh — Can you fill out this form?

Undertegn her. <u>ewn</u>`·nuhr·tayn har — Sign here.

Problems

| There's a problem. | **Jeg har et problem.** yay hahr eht pru·<u>bleh</u>´m |
| I've lost my key/key card. | **Jeg har mistet nøkkelen/nøkkelkortet.** yay hahr <u>mihs</u>`·tuht <u>nurk</u>`·kehl·uhn/<u>nurk</u>`·kehl·kor·tuh |

I've locked myself out of my room.	**Jeg har låst meg ute fra rommet.** *yay hahr lawst may ew`·tuh fra rum´·muh*
There's no hot water/ toilet paper.	**Jeg har ikke varmt vann/toalettpapir.** *yay hahr ihk`·kuh vahrmt vahn/tu·ah·leht´·pah·peer*
The room is dirty.	**Rommet er skittent** *rum´·muh ar shiht`·tuhnt*
There are bugs in our room.	**Det er insekter på rommet vårt.** *deh ar ihn`·sehk·tuhr poh rum´·muh vohrt*
...doesn't work.	**...virker ikke.** *...vihr`·kuhr ihk`·kuh*
Can you fix...?	**Kan du få fikset...?** *kahn dew faw fihk`·suht...*
the air conditioning	**klimaanlegget** *klee´·mah·ahn·lehg·guh*
the fan	**viften** *vihf`·tuhn*
the heat [heating]	**varmen** *vahr`·muhn*
the light	**lyset** *lui´s·uh*
the TV	**TVen** *teh`·veh·uhn*
the toilet	**toalettet** *tu·ah·leht´·tuh*
I'd like to move to another room.	**Jeg vil gjerne flytte til et annet rom.** *yay vihl ya`r·nuh fluit`·tuh tihl eht ahn`·nuht rum*

Checking Out

| When's check-out? | **Når må jeg sjekke ut?** *nohr maw yay shehk`·kuh ewt* |
| Could I leave my bags here until...? | **Kan jeg sette igjen bagasjen min til...?** *kahn yay seht`·tuh ih·yehn´ bah·gah´·shuhn mihn tihl...* |

Can I have an itemized bill/a receipt?	**Kan jeg få en spesifisert regning/kvittering?** *kahn yay faw ehn speh•sih•fih•sehrt´ ray´•ning/ kviht•teh´•rihng*
I think there's a mistake in the bill.	**Jeg tror det er en feil på regningen.** *yay troor deh ar ehn fayl poh ray´•ning•uhn*
I'll pay in cash/by credit card.	**Jeg betaler kontant/med kredittkort.** *yay buh•tah´•luhr kun•tahnt´/meh kreh•diht´•kohrt*

For Grammar, see page 165.

Renting

I've reserved an apartment/a room.	**Jeg har bestilt leilighet/rom.** *yay hahr buh•stihlt´ lay´•li•heht/rum*
My name is...	**Jeg heter...** *yay heh´•tuhr...*
Can I have the key/ key card?	**Kan jeg få nøkkelen/nøkkelkortet?** *kahn yay faw nurk`•kuhl•uhn/ nurk`•kuhl•kor•tuh*
Are there...?	**Fins det...?** *fihns deh...*
dishes	**servise** *sehr•vee´•suh*
pillows	**puter** *pew`•tuhr*
sheets	**lakener** *lah´•kuhn•uhr*
towels	**håndklær** *hohng`•klar*
When/Where do I put out the trash [rubbish] recycling?	**Når/Hvor setter jeg ut søppelet?** *nohr/voor seht´•tuhr yay ewt surp´•puhl•uh*
...is broken.	**...er gått i stykker.** *...ar goht ih stuik´•kuhr*
How does...work?	**Hvordan virker...?** *voor´•dahn vihr´•kuhr*
the air conditioner	**klimaanlegget** *klee´•mah•ahn•lehg•guh*
the dishwasher	**oppvaskmaskinen** *ohp`•vahsk•mah•sheen•uhn*
the freezer	**fryseren** *frui`•suhr•uhn*
the heater	**varmeovnen** *vahr`•muh•ohv•nuhn*
the microwave	**mikrobølgeovnen** *mih´•kru•burl•guh•ohv•nuhn*
the refrigerator	**kjøleskapet** *khur`•luh•skahpuh*

| the stove | **komfyren** kohm•_fui_´•ruhn |
| the washing machine | **vaskemaskinen** _vahs_`•kuh•mah•sh**ee**n•uhn |

Domestic Items

I need...	**Jeg trenger...** yay _trehng_´•uhr...
an adapter	**en adapter** ehn ah•_dahp_´•tuhr
aluminum [kitchen] foil	**aluminiumsfolie** ah•lew•_meen_´•yewms•**fool**•yuh
a bottle opener	**en flaskeåpner** ehn _flahs_`•kuh•awp•nuhr
a broom	**en feiekost** ehn _fay_`•uh•kust
a can opener	**en boksåpner** ehn _bohks_`•awp•nuhr
cleaning supplies	**rengjøringsmidler** _rehn_`•yurr•ihngs•mihd•luhr
a corkscrew	**en korketrekker** ehn _kohr_`•kuh•trehk•kuhr
detergent	**vaskemiddel** _vahs_`•kuh•mihd•duhl
dish detergent	**oppvaskmiddel** _ohp_`•vahsk•mid•duhl
bin bags	**søppelsekker** _surp_`•puhl•sehk•kuhr
a light bulb	**en lyspære** ehn _lui_`s•**pa**•ruh
matches	**fyrstikker** _fuir_`•stihk•kuhr
a mop	**en mopp** ehn mawp
a napkin	**en serviett** ehn sehrv•_yeht_´
paper towels	**husholdningspapir** hews•_hohl_´•nihngs•pah•**peer**
plastic wrap [cling film]	**plastfolie** _plahst_´•**fool**•yuh
a plunger	**en klosettpumpe** ehn klu•seht´•**pum**•puh
scissors	**en saks** ehn sahks
a vacuum cleaner	**en støvsuger** ehn _stur_`v•s**ewg**•uhr

At the Hostel

| Do you have any places left for tonight? | **Har dere noen plasser ledig for i natt?** hahr _deh_`•ruh _noo_`•uhn plahs`•suhr _leh_`•dih fohr ih naht |

Can I have...?	**Kan jeg få...?** *kahn yay faw...*
a single/double room	**et enkeltrom/dobbeltrom** *eht <u>ehng</u>´·kuhlt·rum/ <u>dohb</u>´·buhlt·rum*
a blanket	**et ullteppe** *eht <u>ewl</u>`·tehp·puh*
a pillow	**en pute** *ehn pew`·tuh*
some sheets	**noe sengetøy** *nu·eh sehng·eh·tury*
soap	**såpe** <u>*saw*</u>`·*puh*
towels	**håndklær** <u>*hohng*</u>`·*klar*
What time do you lock up?	**Når stenges ytterdøra?** *nohr <u>stehng</u>`·uhs <u>uit</u>`·tuhr·**dur**·rah*

There are well over 100 hostels throughout Norway run by two different chains: Hostelling International, monitored by **Norske Vandrerhjem** (the Norwegian branch of Hostelling International), and VIP Backpackers Resorts International. Located in cities as well as natural settings like fjords and along the coast, hostels are an inexpensive option. In many cases you may request a private or shared room. The charge per night covers only the cost of the room. Sheets may be brought from home or rented, and meals are separate.

Going Camping

Can we camp here?	**Kan vi campe her?** *kahn vee <u>kehm</u>`•puh har*
Is there a campsite nearby?	**Er det en campingplass i nærheten?** *ar deh ehn <u>kehm</u>´•pihng•plahs ih <u>nar</u>´•heh•tuhn*
What is the charge per day/week?	**Hva koster det per dag/uke?** *vah <u>kohs</u>`•tuhr deh pehr dahg/<u>**ew**</u>`•kuh*
Are there...?	**Fins det...?** *fihns deh...*
cooking facilities	**kokemuligheter** *<u>koo</u>`•kuh•mew•lih•heht•uhr*
electrical outlets	**innlagt strøm** *<u>ihn</u>´•lahkt strurm*
laundry facilities	**vaskemuligheter** *<u>vahs</u>`•kuh•mew•lih•heht•uhr*
showers	**dusj** *dewsh*
tents for rent [hire]	**telt til leie** *tehlt tihl <u>lay</u>`•uh*
Where can I empty the chemical toilet?	**Hvor kan jeg tømme det kjemiske toalettet?** *voor kahn yay <u>turm</u>`•muh de <u>kheh</u>´•mihs•kuh tu•ah•<u>leht</u>´•uh*

YOU MAY SEE...

DRIKKEVANN	drinking water
CAMPING FORBUDT	no camping
BRUK AV ÅPEN ILD FORBUDT	no fires
GRILLING FORBUDT	no barbecues

ESSENTIAL

Where's an internet cafe?	**Hvor finner jeg en internettkafé?** *voor <u>fihn</u>´•nuhr yay ehn <u>ihn</u>´•tuhr•neht•kah•feh*
Can I access the internet/check e-mail?	**Kan jeg bruke internett/sjekke e-post?** *kahn yay <u>brew</u>`•kuh <u>ihn</u>´•tuhr•neht/<u>shehk</u>`•kuh **eh**´•pohst*
How much per hour/half hour?	**Hvor mye er det for en time/halv time?** *voor <u>mui</u>`•uh **ar** deh fohr ehn <u>tee</u>´•muh/hahl <u>tee</u>`•muh*
How do I connect/log on?	**Hvordan kobler jeg meg opp/logger jeg meg inn?** *<u>voor</u>´•dahn <u>kohb</u>`•luhr yay may ohp/<u>lohg</u>`•guhr yay may ihn*
Can I have a phone card?	**Kan jeg få et telefonkort?** *kahn yay faw eht teh•luh•**foon**´•kohrt*
Can I have your phone number?	**Kan jeg få telefonnummeret ditt?** *kahn yay faw teh•luh•**foon**´•num•muhr•uh diht*
Here's my number/e-mail address.	**Her har du nummeret mitt/ e-postadressen min.** *har <u>hahr</u> dew <u>num</u>´•muhr•uh miht/**eh**´•pohst•ahd•rehs•suhn mihn*
Call me.	**Ring meg.** *rihng may*
E-mail me.	**Send meg en e-post.** *sehn may ehn **eh**´•pohst*
Hello. This is...	**Hallo. Dette er...** *hah•<u>loo</u>´ <u>deht</u>`•tuh ar...*
I'd like to speak to...	**Kan jeg få snakke med...?** *kahn yay faw <u>snahk</u>`•kuh meh...*
Can you repeat that?	**Kan du gjenta det?** *kahn dew <u>yehn</u>´•tah deh*
I'll call back later.	**Jeg ringer igjen senere.** *yay <u>rihng</u>`•uhr ih•<u>yehn</u>´ <u>seh</u>`•nuh•ruh*
Goodbye.	**Adjø.** *ahd•<u>yur</u>´*
Where's the post office?	**Hvor er postkontoret?** *voor ar <u>pohst</u>´•kun•toor•uh*
Can I send this to...?	**Kan jeg få sendt dette til...?** *kahn yay faw sehnt <u>deht</u>`•tuh tihl...*

Online

Where's an internet cafe?	**Hvor finner jeg en internettkafé?** *voor* <u>*fihn*</u>´*·nuhr yay ehn* <u>*ihn*</u>´*·tuhr·neht·kah·***feh**
Does it have wireless internet?	**Har den trådløst internett?** *hahr dehn* <u>*traw*</u>`*·lur*st <u>*ihn*</u>´*·tuhr·neht*
What is the WiFi password?	**Hva er WiFi-passordet?** *vah ar vee·fee·pahs·ur·eht*
Is the WiFi free?	**Er WiFi gratis?** *ar vee·fee grah·tihs*
Do you have bluetooth?	**Har dere bluetooth?** *hahr dehr·eh blew·tewth*
How do I turn the computer on/off?	**Hvordan slår jeg på/av datamaskinen?** <u>*voor*</u>´*·dahn* s*lawr yay p***aw***/ah* <u>*dah*</u>´*·tah·mah·sh***ee***n·uhn*
Can I...?	**Kan jeg...?** *kahn yay...*
access the Internet	**bruke internett** <u>*brew*</u>`*·kuh* <u>*ihn*</u>´*·tuhr·neht*
check e-mail	**sjekke e-post** <u>*shehk*</u>`*·kuh* <u>*eh*</u>´*·pohst*
print	**skrive ut** *skree*`*·vuh* ***ewt***
plug in/charge my laptop/iPhone/ iPad/BlackBerry?	**koble til/lade min bærbare maskin/ iPhone/iPad? BlackBerry?** *kawb·leh tihl/lah·deh mihn bar·bahr·eh mah·sheen/ay·foan/ay·pad/blahk·behr·ree*
access Skype?	**bruke Skype** *brew·keh skayp*
How much per hour/ half hour?	**Hvor mye er det for en time/halv time?** *voor* <u>*mui*</u>`*·uh* ***a***r deh fohr ehn* <u>*tee*</u>`*·muh/hahl* <u>*tee*</u>`*·muh*
How do I...?	**Hvordan...?** <u>*voor*</u>´*·dahn...*
connect/disconnect	**kobler jeg meg opp/fra** <u>*kohb*</u>`*·luhr yay may ohp/fr***ah**
log on/off	**logger jeg meg inn/ut** <u>*lohg*</u>`*·guhr jay may ihn/***ewt**
type this symbol	**skriver jeg dette tegnet** <u>*skree*</u>´*·vuhr yay* <u>*deht*</u>`*·tuh* <u>*tay*</u>´*·nuh*
What's your e-mail?	**Hva er e-postadressen din?** *vah ar* <u>*eh*</u>´*·pohst·ahd·rehs·suhn dihn*
My e-mail is...	**E-postadressen min er...** <u>*eh*</u>´*·pohst·ahd·rehs·suhn mihn* ***a***r...*
Do you have a scanner?	**Har dere en skanner?** *hahr dehr·eh ehn skahn·ehr*

YOU MAY SEE...

LUKK	close
SLETT	delete
E-POST	e-mail
AVSLUTT	exit
HJELP	help
INSTANT MESSENGER	instant messenger
INTERNETT	internet
PÅLOGGING	log in
NY (MELDING)	new (message)
PÅ/AV	on/off
ÅPNE	open
SKRIV UT	print
LAGRE	save
SEND	send
BRUKERNAVN/PASSORD	username/password
TRÅDLØST INTERNETT	wireless internet

Social Media

Are you on Facebook/ Twitter?	**Er du på Facebook/Twitter?**	*ar dew paw feis•bewk/ tviht•ehr*
What's your user name?	**Hva er brukernavnet ditt?**	*vah ar brewk•ehr•nahvn•eht diht*
I'll add you as a friend.	**Jeg legger deg til som venn.**	*yay lehg•ehr day tihl sawm vehn*
I'll follow you on Twitter.	**Jeg følger deg på Twitter.**	*yay furl•ehr day paw tviht•ehr*
Are you following...?	**Følger du...?**	*furl•her dew*
I'll put the pictures on Facebook/Twitter.	**Jeg legger ut bildene på Facebook/Twitter.**	*yay lehg•ehr ewt bihl•deh•neh paw feis•bewk/tviht•ehr*

I'll tag you in the pictures.	**Jeg tagger deg i bildene.** *yay tag•ehr day ee bihl•dehn•eh*

Phone

Can I have a phone card/prepaid calling time for… crowns?	**Kan jeg få et telefonkort/ringetid for… kroner?** *kahn yay faw eht teh•luh•<u>**foon**</u>´•kohrt/<u>rihng</u>´•uh•<u>**tee**</u>d fohr… <u>kroo</u>´•n•uhr*
How much?	**Hvor mye koster det?** *voor <u>**mui**</u>´•uh kohs´•tuhr deh*
Where's the pay phone?	**Hvor er telefonautomaten?** *voor ar teh•leh•fun•ev•tu•maht•ehn*
What's the area/ country code for…?	**Hva er retningsnummeret/landkoden til…?** *vah ar <u>reht</u>´•nihngs•num•muhr•uh/<u>lahn</u>´•<u>**kood**</u>•uhn tihl…*
What's the number for Information?	**Hva er nummeret til Opplysningen?** *vah ar <u>num</u>´•muhr•uh tihl ohp•<u>**luis**</u>´•nihng•uhn*
Can I have the number for…?	**Kan jeg få nummeret til…?** *kahn yay faw <u>num</u>´•muhr•uh tihl…*
I'd like to call collect [reverse the charges].	**Jeg vil ringe med noteringsoverføring [mottaker betaler].** *yay vihl rihn•geh meh nut•ehr•ihngs•awv•ehr•furr•ihng mut•ahk•ehr beh•tah•lehr*
My cell [mobile] phone doesn't work here.	**Mobilen min virker ikke her.** *mu•<u>**beel**</u>´•uhn mihn <u>vihr</u>´•kuhr <u>ihk</u>´•kuh har*

In Norway, public phones accept coins, credit cards or **telekort** (prepaid phone cards), which are available at most kiosks, post offices and major train stations.

To call the U.S. or Canada from Norway, dial 00 + 1 + area code + phone number. To call the U.K., dial 00 + 44 + area code (minus the first 0) + phone number. Useful numbers include: information **1880**; operator assistance **1882**.

What network are you on?	**Hvilket nettverk er du på?** *vihl·keht neht·vahrk ar dew paw*
Is it 3G?	**Er det 3G?** *ar deh treh·geh*
I have run out of credit/minutes.	**Jeg gikk tom for kreditt/minutter.** *yay yihk tawm fawr kreh·diht/mihn·ewt·ehr*
Can I buy some credit?	**Kan jeg kjøpe litt kreditt?** *kahn yay shur·peh liht kreh·diht*
Do you have a phone charger?	**Har du en telefonlader?** *Hahr dew ehn teh·leh·fun·lah·dehr*

YOU MAY HEAR...

Hvem er det som ringer? *vehm ar deh sohm rihng`·uhr*	Who's calling?
Et øyeblikk. *eht ury`·uh·blihk*	Hold on.
Jeg skal sette deg over. *yay skahl seht`·tuh day aw`·vuhr*	I'll put you through.
Han/Hun er ute for øyeblikket. *hahn/hewn ar ew`·tuh fohr ury`·uh·blihk·kuh*	He's/She's out at the moment.
Han/Hun kan ikke ta telefonen akkurat nå. *hahn/hewn kahn ihk`·kuh tah teh·luh·foon`·uhn ahk`·kew·raht naw*	He/She can't come to the phone right now.
Vil du legge igjen en beskjed? *vihl dew lehg`·guh ih·yehn` ehn buh·sheh`*	Would you like to leave a message?
Ring igjen senere/om ti minutter. *rihng ih·yehn` seh`·nuh·ruh/ohm tee mihn·ewt`·tuhr*	Call back later/in 10 minutes.
Kan han/hun ringe deg opp? *kahn hahn/hewn rihng`·uh day ohp*	Can he/she call you back?
Hva er nummeret ditt? *vah ar num`·muh·ruh diht*	What's your number?

Can I have your number?	**Kan jeg få nummeret ditt?** *kahn yay faw* <u>*num´*</u>*•muhr•uh diht*
My number is...	**Nummeret mitt er...** <u>*num´*</u>*•muhr•uh miht ar...*
Can you call me?	**Kan du ringe meg?** *kahn dew* <u>*rihng`*</u>*•uh may*
Can you text me?	**Kan du sende meg en tekstmelding?** *kahn dew* <u>*sehn`*</u>*•nuh may ehn* <u>*tehkst´*</u>*•mehl•lihng*
I'll call you.	**Jeg ringer deg.** *yay* <u>*rihng`*</u>*•uhr day*
I'll text you.	**Jeg sender deg en tekstmelding.** *yay* <u>*sehn`*</u>*•nuhr day ehn* <u>*tehkst´*</u>*•mehl•lihng*

Telephone Etiquette

Hello. This is...	**Hallo. Dette er...** *hah•*<u>*loo´*</u> <u>*deht`*</u>*•tuh ar...*
Can I speak to...?	**Kan jeg få snakke med...?** *kahn yay faw* <u>*snahk`*</u>*•kuh meh...*
Extension...	**Linje...** <u>*lihn`*</u>*•yuh...*
Can you speak louder/ more slowly?	**Kan du snakke litt høyere/langsommere?** *kahn dew* <u>*snahk`*</u>*•kuh liht* <u>*hury´*</u>*•uhr•uh/*<u>*lahng´*</u>*•sohm•muhr•uh*
Can you repeat that?	**Kan du gjenta det?** *kahn dew* <u>*yehn´*</u>*•tah deh*
I'll call back later.	**Jeg ringer igjen senere.** *yay* <u>*rihng`*</u>*•uhr ih•*<u>*yehn´*</u> <u>*seh*</u>*eh`•nuh•ruh*
Goodbye.	**Adjø.** *ahd•*<u>*yur´*</u>

Fax

Can I send/receive a fax here?	**Kan jeg sende/motta faks her?** *kahn yay* <u>*sehn`*</u>*•nuh/*<u>*moot´*</u>*•tah fahks har*
What's the fax number?	**Hva er faksnummeret?** *vah ar* <u>*fahks´*</u>*•num•muh•ruh*
Please fax this to...	**Kan du fakse dette til...** *kahn dew* <u>*fahks`*</u>*•uh* <u>*deht`*</u>*•tuh tihl...*

Post

| Where's the post office/ mailbox [postbox]? | **Hvor finner jeg et postkontor/en postkasse?** *voor* <u>*fihn´*</u>*•nuhr yay eht* <u>*pohst´*</u>*•kun•too*r*/ehn* <u>*pohst´*</u>*•kahs•suh* |

A stamp for this letter/ postcard, please.	**Et frimerke til dette brevet/kortet, takk.** *eht free´·mehrk·uh til deht`·tuh breh´·vuh/kohr´·tuh tahk*
How much?	**Hvor mye koster det?** *voor mui`·uh kohs`·tuhr deh*
I'd like to send this by airmail/express mail.	**Jeg vil gjerne sende dette med flypost/ekspress.** *yay vihl ya`r·nuh sehn`·nuh deht`·tuh meh flui·pohst/ ehks·prehs´*
Can I have a receipt?	**Kan jeg få kvittering?** *kahn yay faw kviht·teh´·rihng*

YOU MAY HEAR...

Kan du fylle ut en tolldeklarasjon? *kahn dew fuil´·luh ewt ehn tohl`·deh·klah·rah·shoon*	Can you fill out the customs declaration form?
Hva er verdien? *vah ar vehr·dee´·uhn*	What's the value?
Hva er det inni? *vah ar deh ihn`·ih*	What's inside?

Norwegian post offices are generally open Monday to Friday from 8:00 a.m. to 4:00 p.m. and Saturday from 9:00 a.m. to 1:00 p.m. Mailboxes are painted red and display the trumpet symbol of the post office.

Food & Drink

ESSENTIAL

Can you recommend a good restaurant/bar? **Kan du anbefale en bra restaurant/bar?** *kahn dew ahn´·buh·fah·luh ehn brah rehs·tew·rahng´/bahr*

Is there a traditional Norwegian/an inexpensive restaurant near here? **Fins det en typisk norsk/billig restaurant i nærheten?** *fihns deh ehn tui´·pihsk nohrsk/bihl`·lih rehs·tew·rahng´ ih nar´·heh·tuhn*

A table for... **Et bord til...** *eht boor tihl...*

Could we have a table here/there? **Kan vi få et bord her/der?** *kahn vee faw eht eht boor har/dar*

Could we have a table in the corner? **Kan vi få et hjørnebord?** *kahn vee faw eht eht yur`n·uh·boor*

I'm waiting for someone. **Jeg venter på noen.** *yay vehn`·tuhr poh noo`·uhn*

Where is the restroom [toilet]? **Hvor er toalettet?** *voor ar tu·ah·leht´·tuh*

Can I have a menu? **Kan jeg få se menyen?** *kahn yay faw seh meh·nui´·uhn*

What do you recommend? **Hva kan du anbefale?** *vah kahn dew ahn´·buh·fah·luh*

I'd like... **Jeg vil gjerne ha...** *yay vihl ya`r·nuh hah...*

Can I have more...? **Kan jeg få litt mer...?** *kahn yay faw liht mehr...*

Enjoy your meal! **God appetitt!** *gu ahp·puh·tiht´*

Can I have the check [bill]? **Kan jeg få regningen?** *kahn yay faw ray`·nihng·uhn*

Is service included? **Er service inkludert?** *ar surr´·vihs ing·klew·dehrt´*

Can I pay by credit card? **Kan jeg betale med kredittkort?** *kahn yay buh·tah´·luh meh kreh·diht´·kohrt*

| Can I have a receipt? | **Kan jeg få kvittering?** kahn yay faw kviht•_teh_´•rihng |
| Thank you. | **Takk.** tahk |

Where to Eat

Can you recommend...?	**Kan du anbefale...?** kahn dew <u>ahn</u>´•buh•**fah**•luh...
a restaurant	**en restaurant** ehn rehs•tew•_rahng_´
a bar	**en bar** ehn bahr
a cafe	**en kafé** ehn kah•<u>feh</u>´
an authentic/a non-touristy restaurant	**en autentisk/turistfri restaurant** ehn ev•tehn•tihsk/tew•rihst•free rehs•tew•rahng
a cheap restaurant	**en billig restaurant** ehn bihl•ih rehs•tew•rahng
an expensive restaurant	**en dyr restaurant** ehn dyr rehs•tew•rahng
a fast-food place	**en hurtigmatrestaurant** <u>ehn hewr</u>`•tih•maht•rehs•tew•rahng
a restaurant with a good view	**en restaurant med god utsikt** ehn rehs•tew•rahng meh gu ewt•sihkt

Reservations & Preferences

I'd like to reserve a table...	**Jeg vil gjerne bestille et bord...** yay vihl <u>ya</u>`r•nuh buhs•<u>tihl</u>´•luh eht boor...
for four	**til fire** tihl <u>fee</u>`•ruh
for this evening	**til i kveld** tihl ih kvehl
for tomorrow at...	**til i morgen klokken...** tihl ih <u>maw</u>`•ruhn <u>klohk</u>`•kuhn...
A table for two, please.	**Et bord til to, takk.** eht boor´ tihl too tahk
We have a reservation.	**Vi har bestilt bord.** vee hahr buhs•<u>tihlt</u>´ boor
My name is...	**Jeg heter...** yay <u>heh</u>`•tuhr...

YOU MAY SEE...

INNGANGSPENGER	cover charge
DAGENS MENY	menu of the day
SPESIALITETER	specials
TIPS (IKKE) INKLUDERT	service (not) included

Could we have…? **Kan vi få et…?** *kahn vee faw…*

  a table here/there **et bord her/der** *eht boor har/dar*

  a table in the corner **et hjørnebord** *eht yur`·nuh·boor*

  a table by the **vindusbord** *vihn`·dews·boor*
  window

Can we sit… **Kan vi sitte…** *kahn vee siht·eh*

  outside **ute** *ewte*

  in the shade **i skyggen** *ee shyh·gehn*

  in the sun **i solen** *ee sul·ehn*

  in a non-smoking **i et røykfritt område** *ee eht ruryk·friht um·raw·deh*
  area

Where is the restroom **Hvor er toalettet?** *voor ar tu·ah·leht´·tuh*
[toilet]?

For Time, see page 171.

How to Order

Waiter/Waitress!	**Servitør!** *ser·vih·turr´*	
We're ready to order.	**Vi er klare til å bestille.** *vee ar klah`·ruh tihl aw buhs·tihl´·luh*	
Can I have the wine list?	**Kan jeg få se vinkartet?** *kahn yay faw seh veen`·kahr·tuh*	
I'd like...	**Jeg vil gjerne ha...** *yay vihl ya`r·nuh hah...*	
a bottle of...	**en flaske...** *ehn flahs`·kuh...*	
a carafe of...	**en karaffel...** *ehn kah·rahf´·fuhl...*	
a glass of...	**et glass...** *eht glahs...*	
Can I have a menu?	**Kan jeg få se menyen?** *kahn yay faw seh meh·nui´·uhn*	

YOU MAY HEAR...

Har dere bestilt bord? *hahr deh·ruh buhs·tihlt´ boor*	Do you have a reservation?
Hvor mange? *voor mahn·geh*	How many?
Røyk eller røykfritt? *ruryk ehl·ehr ruryk·friht*	Smoking or non-smoking?
Er dere klare til å bestille? *ar deh·ruh klah´·ruh tihl aw buhs·tihl´·luh*	Are you ready to order?
Hva skal det være? *vah skahl deh va`·ruh*	What would you like?
Jeg anbefaler... *yay ahn·beh·fahl·ehr*	I recommend...
God appetitt. *gu ahp·puh·tiht´*	Enjoy your meal.

Do you have…?	**Har dere…?**	*hahr deh`·ruh…*
a menu in English	**en meny på engelsk**	*ehn meh·nui´ poh ehng´·ehlsk*
a set menu	**en fast meny**	*ehn fahst meh·nui´*
a children's menu	**en barnemeny**	*ehn bahr`·nuh·meh·nui*
What do you recommend?	**Hva kan du anbefale?**	*vah kahn dew ahn´·buh·fah·luh*
What's this?	**Hva er dette?**	*vah ar deht`·tuh*
What's in it?	**Hva inneholder den/det?**	*vah ihn`·nuh·hawl·luhr dehn/deh*
Is it spicy?	**Er den/det sterkt krydret?**	*ar dehn/deh sterkt kruid`·ruht*
rare	**råstekt**	*raw`·stehkt*
medium	**medium stekt**	*meh´·dih·ewm stehkt*
well-done	**godt stekt**	*goht stehkt*
Can I have more…?	**Kan jeg få litt mer…?**	*kahn yay faw liht mehr…*
With/Without…	**Med/Uten…**	*meh/ew`·tuhn…*
I can't eat…	**Jeg tåler ikke…**	*yay taw´·luhr ihk`·kuh…*
It's to go [take away].	**Jeg tar det med meg.**	*yay tahr´ deh meh may*

For Grammar, see page 165.

Cooking Methods

baked	**bakt** *bahkt*
boiled	**kokt** *kukt*
braised	**braisert** *brahs·seh´rt*
breaded	**panert** *pah·neh´rt*
creamed	**fløtegratinert** *flur`·tuh·grah·tih·nehrt*
diced	**i terninger** *ih ter`·nihng·uhr*
fried	**stekt** *stehkt*
grilled (broiled)	**grillet** *grihl`·luht*
poached	**pochert** *pu·sheh´rt*
roasted	**ovnsstekt** *ohvns`·stehkt*
sautéed	**sautert** *soh·teh´rt*
smoked	**røkt** *rurkt*
steamed	**dampet** *dahm`·puht*
stewed	**stuet** *stew`·uht*
stuffed	**fylt** *fuilt*

Dietary Requirements

I'm…	**Jeg er…** *yay ar…*
a diabetic	**diabetiker** *dih·ah·beh´·tihk·uhr*
lactose intolerant	**laktoseintolerant** *lahk·too`·suh·ihn·toh·luh·rahnt*
a vegetarian	**vegetarianer** *veh·guh·tahr·ih·ah´·nuhr*
vegan	**veganer** *veh·gah·nehr*
I'm allergic to…	**Jeg er allergisk mot…** *yay ar ah·lehr´·gihsk moot…*
I can't eat…	**Jeg kan ikke spise…** *yay kahn ihk`·kuh spee`·suh…*
dairy	**melkeprodukter** *mehl`·kuh·pru·dewk·tuhr*
gluten	**gluten** *glew´·tuhn*
nuts	**nøtter** *nurt´·tuhr*
pork	**svinekjøtt** *svee`·nuh·khurt*
shellfish	**skalldyr** *skahl`·duir*
spicy foods	**sterkt krydret mat** *sterkt kruid`·ruht maht*
wheat	**hvete** *veh´·tuh*

Is it halal/kosher?	**Er maten halal/kosher?** *ar <u>mah</u>´t·uhn hahl·<u>ahl</u>´/ <u>kohsh</u>´·uhr*
Do you have...?	**Har dere?** *hahr dehr·eh*
skimmed milk	**skummet melk** *sku·meht mehlk*
whole milk	**helmelk** *hehl·mehlk*
soya milk	**soyamelk** *soy·ah·mehlk*

Dining with Children

Do you have children's portions?	**Har dere barneporsjoner?** *hahr d<u>eh</u>´·ruh <u>bahr</u>´·nuh·poor·sh<u>oo</u>n·uhr*
Can I have a highchair/child's seat?	**Kan jeg få en babystol/barnestol?** *kahn yay faw ehn <u>beh</u>´·bih·st<u>oo</u>l/<u>bahr</u>´·nuh·st<u>oo</u>l*
Where can I feed/ change the baby?	**Hvor kan jeg amme/bytte på babyen?** *voor kahn yay ah´·muh/<u>buit</u>´·tuh poh <u>beh</u>´·bih·uhn*
Can you warm this?	**Kan du varme opp denne?** *kahn dew <u>vahr</u>´·muh ohp <u>dehn</u>´·nuh*

How to Complain

How much longer will our food be?	**Hvor lenge drøyer det med maten?** *vur <u>lehng</u>´·uh <u>drury</u>´·uhr deh meh <u>maht</u>´·uhn*
We can't wait any longer.	**Vi kan ikke vente lenger.** *vee kahn <u>ihk</u>´·kuh <u>vehn</u>´·tuh <u>lehng</u>´·uhr*
We're leaving.	**Vi drar.** *vee dr<u>a</u>hr*
That's not what I ordered.	**Dette er ikke det jeg bestilte.** *<u>deht</u>´·tuh ar <u>ihk</u>´·kuh deh yay buh·<u>stihl</u>´·tuh*
I asked for...	**Jeg ba om...** *yay bah um...*
I can't eat this.	**Jeg kan ikke spise dette.** *yay kahn <u>ihk</u>´·kuh sp<u>ee</u>´·suh deht´·tuh*

This is too…	**Det er for…** *deh ar fohr…*
cold/hot	**kaldt/varmt** *kahlt/varmt*
salty/spicy	**salt/krydret** *sahlt/<u>kruid</u>·ruht*
tough/bland	**seigt/mildt** *saykt/mihlt*
This isn't clean/fresh.	**Dette er ikke rent/ferskt.** <u>deht</u>`·tuh ar <u>ihk</u>`·kuh rehnt/ferskt

Paying

Can I have the check [bill]?	**Kan jeg får regningen?** *kahn yay faw <u>rayn</u>`·nihng·uhn*
We'd like to pay separately.	**Vi vil gjerne betale hver for oss.** *vee vihl yar`·nuh buh·<u>tah</u>´·luh var fohr ohs*
It's all together.	**Det er for alt sammen.** *deh ar fohr ahlt <u>sam</u>·muhn*
Is service included?	**Er service inkludert?** *ar <u>surr</u>´·vihs ihng·klew·<u>dehrt</u>´*
What's this amout for?	**Hva står dette beløpet for?** *vah stawr <u>deht</u>`·tuh buh·<u>lur</u>´·puh fohr*
I didn't have that. I had…	**Jeg spiste ikke det. Jeg spiste…** *yay <u>spihs</u>`·tuh <u>ihk</u>`·kuh deh yay <u>spihs</u>`·tuh…*
Can I pay by credit card?	**Kan jeg betale med kredittkort?** *kahn yay buh·<u>tah</u>´·luh meh kreh·<u>diht</u>´·kort*
Can I have an itemized bill/a receipt?	**Kan jeg få en spesifisert regning/en kvittering?** *kahn yay faw ehn speh·sih·fih·<u>seh</u>´rt <u>ray</u>`·nihng/ehn kviht·<u>teh</u>´·rihng*
That was a very good meal.	**Maten smakte veldig godt.** <u>maht</u>´·uhn <u>smahk</u>`·tuh <u>vehl</u>`·dih goht
I've already paid.	**Jeg har allerede betalt.** *yay hahr ahl·eh·rehd·eh beh·tahlt*

A 10-15% service charge is typically included in most restaurant bills, though wait staff often receive an extra 5-10% tip.

Meals & Cooking

Breakfast

appelsinjuice *ahp·puhl·see´n·yews*	orange juice
appelsinmarmelade *ahp·puhl·see´n·mahr·muh·lah·duh*	orange marmalade
brød *brur*	bread
bløtkokt/hardkokt egg *blur`t·kukt/ hah`r·kukt ehg*	soft-boiled/hard-boiled eggs
egg og bacon/skinke *ehg aw bay´·kuhn/ shihng`·kuh*	eggs with bacon/ham
eggerøre *ehg`·guh·rur·ruh*	scrambled eggs
frokostblanding *froo´·kohst·blahn·nihng*	cereal
grapefruktjuice *grehp´·frewkt·yews*	grapefruit juice
havregrøt *hahv`·ruh·grurt*	oatmeal [porridge]
honning *hohn`·nihng*	honey
juice *yews*	fruit juice
svart/koffeinfri kaffe *svahrt/ kohf·fuh·ee´n· free kahf´·fuh*	black/decaffeinated coffee
kaffe med melk/fløte *kahf´·fuh meh mehlk/flur`·tuh*	coffee with milk/cream
omelett *oh·muh·leht´*	omelet
ost *ust*	cheese
ristet brød *rihs`·tuht brur*	toast
rundstykke *rewn´·stuik·kuh*	roll
smør *smurr*	butter
speilegg *spayl`·ehg*	fried egg
syltetøy *suil`·tuh·tury*	jam
te med melk/sitron *teh meh mehlk/ siht·roo´n*	tea with milk/lemon
varm sjokolade *vahrm shu·ku·lah`·duh*	hot chocolate

varmt vann *varmt vahn*	hot water
yoghurt *yoo´·gewrt*	yogurt

Frokost (breakfast) is usually eaten early and consists of coffee or tea and **smørbrød** (open-faced sandwiches) and perhaps cereal. **Lunsj** (lunch) is typically a light meal and may consist of a simple **matpakke** (open-faced sandwich brought from home). **Middag** (dinner) is often the only hot meal of the day. If **middag** is eaten early, then **aftens** (a late night snack), consisting of bread or crackers with butter or cheese and cold cuts, is eaten to get through the night without going hungry.

Appetizers

blåskjell *blaw`·shehl*	mussels
fenalår *feh`·nah·lawr*	cured leg of mutton
ferske reker *fehrs`·kuh reh`·kuhr*	unshelled shrimp [prawns]
fiskekabaret *fihs`·kuh·kah·bah·reh*	assorted seafood and vegetables in aspic
gåselever *gaw`·suh·leh·vuhr*	goose liver

gravlaks _grahv_`·lahks	cured salmon flavored with dill
hummer _hum_´·muhr	lobster
kamskjell _kahm_`·shehl	scallop
kaviar kah·vih·**ah**´r	caviar
krabbe _krahb_`·buh	crab
laks lahks	salmon
rakørret _rahk_`·urr·ruht	specially processed, salt-cured and fermented trout
rekecocktail _reh_`·kuh·kohk·tayl	shrimp [prawn] cocktail
røkelaks _rur_`·kuh·lahks	smoked salmon
sildebrikke _sihl_`·luh·brihk·kuh	a variety of herring, served with bread and butter
skinke _shihng_`·kuh	ham
spekepølse _speh_`·kuh·purl·suh	smoked, cured sausage
spekeskinke _speh_`·kuh·shihng·kuh	smoked, cured ham
sursild _sewr_´sihl	marinated herring
østers _urs_´·tehrs	oysters

Soup

aspargessuppe ahs·_pahr_´·guhs·sewp·puh	asparagus soup
betasuppe _beh_`·tah·sewp·puh	thick meat and vegetable soup
blomkålsuppe _blohm_´·kawl·sewp·puh	cauliflower soup
buljong bewl·_yohng_´	consommé
fiskesuppe _fihs_`·kuh·sewp·puh	fish soup
fransk løksuppe frahnsk _lur_`k·sewp·puh	French onion soup
grønnsaksuppe _grurn_`·**sahk**·sewp·puh	vegetable soup
gul ertesuppe gewl _er_`·tuh·sewp·puh	yellow pea soup
hummersuppe _hum_`·muhr·sewp·puh	lobster soup
kjøttsuppe _khurt_`·sewp·puh	meat soup

løksuppe _lur`k•sewp•puh_ — onion soup
neslesuppe _nehs`-luh-sewp•puh_ — nettle soup
oksehalesuppe _ohk`-suh-hah-luh-sewp•puh_ — oxtail soup
sellerisuppe _seh-luh-ree´-sewp•puh_ — celery soup
sjampinjongsuppe — button mushroom soup
shahm•pihn•yohng´-sewp•puh
soppsuppe _sohp`-sewp•puh_ — field mushroom soup
tomatsuppe _tu•mah´t-sewp•puh_ — tomato soup

> Norwegian cuisine features a wide range of soups, which are
> often eaten with **flatbrød** (a thin, barley and wheat or barley
> and rye cracker); this is a common starter. **Fiskesuppe** (fish soup)
> is very popular along the coast. Other traditional soups involve meat,
> such as **betasuppe** (meat and vegetable soup), or vegetables, like **gul
> ertesuppe** (yellow pea soup).

Fish & Seafood

abbor _ahb`•bohr_ — perch
akkar _ahk`•kahr_ — squid
ansjos _ahn•shoo´s_ — anchovies or marinated
sprats
blåskjell _blaw`•shehl_ — mussels
blekksprut _blehk`•sprewt_ — octopus
brasme _brahs`•muh_ — bream
breiflabb _bray`•flahb_ — angler, also called frogfish or
goosefish
dampet ørret _dahm`•puht urr`•ruht_ — poached trout
fisk _fihsk_ — fish
fiskeboller _fihs`•kuh•bohl•luhr_ — fish balls

fiskekaker _fihs`·kuh·kah·kuhr_	fried fish cakes
fiskepudding _fihs`·kuh·pewd·dihng_	fish pudding
flyndre _fluin`·druh_	flounder
fritert flyndrefilet _friht·eh´rt fluin`·druh·fih·leh_	deep fried flounder fillet
gjedde _yehd`·duh_	pike
gravlaks _grah`v·lahks_	cured salmon flavored with dill
hellefisk _hehl`·luh·fihsk_	halibut
hummer _hum´·muhr_	lobster
hvitting _viht`·tihng_	whiting
hyse _hui`·suh_	haddock (western Norway)
kamskjell _kahm`·shel_	scallop
karpe _kahr`·puh_	carp
klippfisk _klihp´·fihsk_	salted and dried fish
kokt torsk _kukt tohrsk_	poached cod
kokt ørret _kukt urr`·ruht_	poached trout
kolje _kohl`·yuh_	haddock (eastern Norway)
krabbe _krahb`·buh_	crab
kreps _krehps_	freshwater crayfish
kveite _kvay`·tuh_	halibut
laks _lahks_	salmon

lutefisk _lew`·tuh·fihsk_	stockfish soaked in lye
lysing _lui`·sihng_	hake
makrell _mahk·rehl´_	mackerel
piggvar _pihg`·vahr_	turbot
plukkfisk _pluk´·fihsk_	stewed codfish
regnbueørret _rayn`·bew·uh·urr·ruht_	rainbow trout
reker _reh`·kuhr_	shrimp [prawns]
rogn _rohngn_	roe
rødspette _rur`·speht·tuh_	plaice
sardell _sar·dehl´_	canned anchovy
sardin _sar·dee´n_	sardine
sei _say_	pollock
sik _seek_	whitefish
sild _sihl_	herring
sjømat _shur`·maht_	seafood
sjøørret _shur`·urr·ruht_	sea trout
sjøtunge _shur`·tung·uh_	sole
skalldyr _skahl`·duir_	shellfish
spekesild _speh`·kuh·sihl_	salted herring
steinbit _stayn`·beet_	catfish
stør _sturr_	sturgeon
størje _sturr`·yuh_	tuna
torsk _tohrsk_	cod
tunfisk _tew`n·fihsk_	tuna
tørrfisk _turr´·fihsk_	stockfish
uer _ew`·uhr_	rosefish
ørret _urr`·ruht_	trout
østers _urs´·tehrs_	oysters
åbor _aw`·bohr_	perch
ål _awl_	eel

Meat & Poultry

and *ahn*	duck
bacon <u>*bay*</u>´·*kuhn*	bacon
benløse fugler <u>*beh*</u>`n·*lurs*·uh *few*`l·*uhr*	fried, rolled and stuffed slices of veal or beef
biff *bihf*	beef steak
biff med løk *bihf meh l**u**rk*	thick beef steak topped with fried onion
broiler <u>*broi*</u>´·*luhr*	chicken
brun lapskaus *brewn* <u>*lahps*</u>´·*kevs*	Norwegian stew in brown gravy
dyrestek <u>*dui*</u>`·*ruh*·*stehk*	roast venison
elg *ehlg*	moose
elgbiff <u>*ehlg*</u>`·*bihf*	moose steak
elgfilet <u>*ehlg*</u>`·*fih*·*leh*	moose fillet
elgstek <u>*ehlg*</u>`·*stehk*	roast moose
fårestek <u>*faw*</u>`·*ruh*·*stehk*	roast leg of mutton or lamb
fårekjøtt <u>*faw*</u>`·*ruh*·*khurt*	mutton
fårikål <u>*faw*</u>´·*rih*·*kawl*	mutton or lamb in cabbage stew
fasan *fah*·<u>*sah*</u>´*n*	pheasant
gås *gaws*	goose
hare <u>*hah*</u>`·*ruh*	hare
hjort *yohrt*	deer
høne <u>*hur*</u>`·*nuh*	hen
hvalbiff *vahl*`·*bihf*	whale steak
kalkun *kahl*·<u>*kew*</u>´*n*	turkey
kalvebrissel <u>*kahl*</u>`·*vuh*·*brihs*·*suhl*	calf's sweetbread
kalvekjøtt <u>*kahl*</u>`·*vuh*·*khurt*	veal
kalvelever <u>*kahl*</u>`·*vuh*·*lehv*·*vuhr*	calf's liver
kanin *kah*·<u>*nee*</u>´*n*	rabbit

karbonade *kahr·bu·nah`·duh* — hamburger
kjøttboller *khurt* — meatballs
kjøttkaker *khurt`·kahk·uhr* — small hamburgers
kjøttpudding *khurt`·pud·dihng* — meatloaf
knoke *knoo`·kuh* — bone
kotelett *koh·tuh·leht´* — chop
kylling *khuil`·lihng* — chicken
lammekjøtt *lahm`·muh·khurt* — lamb
lapskaus *lahps´·kehvs* — Norwegian stew with meat, potatoes and root vegetables
lever *lehv´·vuhr* — liver
lys lapskaus *luis lahps´·kehvs* — Norwegian stew with diced, salted boiled pork
medisterkaker *meh·dihs´·tuhr·kah·kuhr* — small pork and beef hamburgers
medisterpølse *meh·dihs´·tuhr·purl·suh* — pork and beef sausage
mørbradstek *mur`r·brahd·stehk* — roast sirloin
nyrer *nui`·ruhr* — kidneys
oksebryst *ohk`·suh·bruist* — beef brisket
oksekjøtt *ohk`·suh·khurt* — beef
okserulader *ohk`·suh·rewl·lah·duhr* — braised beef rolls
oksestek *ohk`·suh·stehk* — roast beef
orrfugl *ohr`·fewl* — black grouse, a woodland bird
pinnekjøtt *pihn`·nuh·khurt* — salted and dried mutton ribs steamed on twigs
pytt i panne *puit·ih·pah`·nuh* — hash or meat and vegetables
pølse *purl`·suh* — sausage
rådyr *raw`·duir* — roe-deer
rapphøne *rahp`·hur·nuh* — partridge
reinsdyr *rayns´·duir* — reindeer

ribbe _rihb`·buh_	spareribs
rype _rui`·puh_	grouse, a mountain bird
skinke _shihng`·kuh_	ham
spekeskinke _speh`·kuh·shihng·kuh_	smoked, cured ham
stek _stehk_	roast (beef, reindeer, moose, etc.)
svinekjøtt _svee`·nuh·khurt_	pork
svor _svoor_	bacon rind [crackling]
sylte _suil`·tuh_	head cheese [brawn]
tartarbiff _tahr·tah´r·bihf_	steak tartare
T-benstek _teh´·behn·stehk_	T-bone steak
vaktel _vahk´·tuhl_	quail
villand _vihl`·lahn_	wild duck
wienerschnitzel _vee´·nuhr·shniht·suhl_	breaded veal cutlet

Vegetables & Staples

agurk _ah·gewr´k_	cucumber
anisfrø _ah´·nihs·frur_	aniseed
artisjokker _ar·tih·shohk´·kuhr_	artichokes
asparges _ahs·pahr´·guhs_	asparagus
aubergine _aw·buhr·shee´n_	eggplant [aubergine]
basilikum _bah·see´·lih·kewm_	basil
blomkål _blohm´·kawl_	cauliflower
bønner _burn`·nuhr_	beans
brokkoli _brohk´·koh·lih_	broccoli
dill _dihl_	dill
erter _ehr´·tuhr_	peas
gresskar _grehs`·kahr_	pumpkin
gressløk _grehs`·lurk_	chives
grønnkål _grurn´·kawl_	kale

gulrøtter _gew`l_·rurt·tuhr	carrots
hodesalat _hoo`_·duh·sah·_laht_	lettuce
hvitløk _vee´t_·_lurk_	garlic
ingefær _ihng´_·uh·_far_	ginger
kål _kawl_	cabbage
kanel kah·_neh´l_	cinnamon
kantareller kahn·tah·_rehl´_·luhr	chanterelle mushrooms
kapers _kah´_·puhrs	capers
karri _kahr´_·rih	curry seasoning
karve _kahr`_·vuh	caraway seeds
kokte poteter _kuk`_·tuh pu·_teh´t_·uhr	boiled potatoes
komler/komper _kum`_·luhr/_kum`_·puhr	potato dumplings
linser _lihn`_·suhr	lentils
løk _lurk_	onions
mais _mies_	corn
maiskolbe _mies´_·kohl·buh	corn on the cob
nellik _nehl´_·lihk	clove
nepe _neh`_·puh	turnip
nudler _newd´_·luhr	noodles
nypoteter _nui`_·pu·_teht_·uhr	new potatoes
paprika _pahp´_·rih·kah	sweet pepper
persille pehr·_sihl´_·luh	parsley

pommes frites *pohm friht*	French fries [chips]
potet *pu·teh´t*	potato
potetgull *pu·teh´t·gewl*	potato chips [crisps]
potetkroketter *pu·teh´t·krohk·keht·tuhr*	potato croquettes
potetmos *pu·teh´t·moos*	mashed potatoes
potetsalat *pu·teh´t·sah·laht*	potato salad
purre *pewr`·ruh*	leeks
raspeball *rahs´·puh·bahl*	potato dumplings
reddiker *rehd´·dihk·kuhr*	radishes
ris *rees*	rice
rosenkål *roo´·suhn·kawl*	Brussels sprouts
rødbeter *rur`·beh·tuhr*	beet [beetroot]
rødkål *rur´·kawl*	red cabbage
salat *sah·lah´t*	salad
salvie *sahl·vee`·uh*	sage
selleri *sehl·luhr·ee´*	celery
sildeball *sihl`·luh·bahl*	potato dumplings filled with minced salted herring
stekte poteter *stehk`·tuh pu·teh´t·uhr*	sautéed potatoes
stuede poteter *stew`·eh·duh pu·teh´t·uhr*	potatoes in a white sauce
sjampinjonger *sham·pihn·yohng´·uhr*	button mushrooms
sopp *sohp*	mushrooms
spinat *spih·nah´t*	spinach
surkål *sew´r·kawl*	coleslaw
sylteagurk *suil`·tuh·ah·gewrk*	pickle
timian *tee´·mih·ahn*	thyme
tomater *tu·maht´·uhr*	tomatoes

Fruit

ananas *ahn´·nah·nahs*	pineapple
appelsin *ahp·puhl·see´n*	orange
aprikos *ahp·rih·koo´s*	apricot

banan bah-_nah_´n	banana
bjørnebær _byur_`-nuh-bar	blackberries
blåbær _blaw_`-bar	blueberries
bringebær _brihng_´-uh-bar	raspberries
dadler _dahd_´-luhr	dates
druer _drew_`-uhr	grapes
einebær _ay_`-nuh-bar	juniper berries
eple _ehp_`-luh	apple
fersken _fehrs_´-kuhn	peach
fikener _fee_´-kuhn-uhr	figs
grapefrukt _grehp_´-frewkt	grapefruit
hasselnøtter _hahs_´-suhl-nurt-tuhr	hazelnuts
jordbær _yoo_´r-bar	strawberries
kastanjer kahs-_tahn_´-yuhr	chestnuts
kirsebær _khihr_´-suh-bar	cherries
kokosnøtt _kuk_´-kus-nurt	coconut
korinter ku-_rihn_´-tuhr	currants
mandarin mahn-dah-_ree_´n	tangerine
mandler _mahn_´d-luhr	almonds
markjordbær _mahr_`k-yoor-bar	wild strawberries
melon meh-_loo_´n	melon

molter/multer _mohl_`·tuhr/mewl`·tuhr	arctic cloudberries
moreller mu·_rehl_`·luhr	morello cherries
nektarin nehk·tah·_ree_´n	nectarine
nøtter _nurt_´·tuhr	nuts
peanøtter _pee_´·ah·nurt·tuhr	peanuts
plommer _plum_`·muhr	plums
pære _pa_`·ruh	pear
rabarbra rah·_bahr_´·brah	rhubarb
rips rihps	red currants
rognebær _rohng_`·nuh·bar	rowanberries
rosiner ru·_see_´·nuhr	raisins
sitron siht·_roo_´n	lemon
solbær _soo_`l·bar	black currants
stikkelsbær _stihk_´·kuhls·bar	gooseberries
svisker _svihs_`·kuhr	prunes
tranebær _trah_´·nuh·bar	cranberries
tyttebær _tuit_´·tuh·bar	lingonberry
valnøtter _vahl_`·nurt·tuhr	walnuts
vannmelon _vahn_`·meh·_loo_n	watermelon

Cheese

ekte geitost _ehk_`·tuh _yayt_`·ust	goat cheese
fløtemysost _flur_`·tuh·_muis_·ust	mild and sweet cow's milk cheese
gammelost _gahm_`·muhl·ust	pungent cheese made with skimmed milk
gudbrandsdalsost _gewd_`·brahns·_dahl_s·ust	cow and goat's milk cheese
jarlsbergost _yahrls_´·behrg·ust	mild, slightly sweet, semi-hard cheese
normannaost noor·_mahn_´·nah·ust	blue-veined cow's milk cheese
ridderost _rihd_´·duhr·ust	semi-hard cheese with nutty flavor

Dessert

bløtkake _blur`t·kah·kuh_	layer cake
fruktkompott _frewkt´·kohm·poht_	stewed fruit
hoffdessert _hohf´·dehs·sar_	layers of meringue and whipped cream, topped with chocolate sauce and toasted almonds
is _ees_	ice cream
karamellpudding _kah·rah·mehl´·pewd·dihng_	creme caramel
krem _krehm_	whipped cream
mandelkake _mahn´·duhl·kah·kuh_	almond cake
molter/multer med krem _mohl´·tuhr/mewl` tuhr meh krehm_	arctic cloudberries with whipped cream
pære Belle Helene _pa`·ruh behl heh·leh´n_	poached pears with vanilla ice cream and chocolate
pannekaker _pahn`·nuh·kah·kuhr_	pancakes
riskrem _ree´s·krehm_	creamed rice
rødgrøt med fløte _rur`·grurt meh flur`·tuh_	berry compote with cream
sjokoladepudding _shu·ku·lah`·duh·pewd·dihng_	chocolate pudding
sorbett _sohr·beht´_	sorbet
sufflé _sewf·leh´_	soufflé
terte _tehr`·tuh_	fruit cake
tilslørte bondepiker _tihl´·slurr·tuh bun´·nuh·pee·kuhr_	layers of stewed apples, cookie [biscuit] crumbs, and whipped cream
vafler med syltetøy _vahf´·luhr meh suil`·tuh·tury_	waffles with jam
vaniljesaus _vah·nihl`·yuh·sevs_	vanilla sauce
varm eplekake med krem _vahrm ehp`·luh·kah·kuh meh krehm_	hot apple pie with whipped cream

Sauces & Condiments

ketchup	**ketchup** *kat•shewp*
mustard	**sennep** *sehn•ehp*
pepper	**pepper** _pehp`_•*puhr*
salt	**salt** *sahlt*

At the Market

Where are the carts [trolleys]/baskets?	**Hvor er handlevognene/handlekurvene?** *voor **ar** hahn`d•luh•vohng•nuh•nuh/ hahn`d•luh•kewr•vuh•nuh*
Where is…?	**Hvor er…?** *voor **ar**…*
Can I have some of that/those?	**Kan jeg få litt av det/dem?** *kahn yay f**aw** liht a deh/ dehm*
Can I taste it?	**Kan jeg smake?** *kahn yay sm**ah**`•kuh*

In Norway, there are a few large supermarket chains, such as Rimi, Rema and Kiwi, in addition to many local mini-markets. Keep in mind that supermarkets do not accept credit cards, so remember to bring cash when you go shopping for groceries.

Measurements in Europe are metric - and that applies to the weight of food too. If you tend to think in pounds and ounces, it's worth brushing up on what the metric equivalent is before you go shopping for fruit and veg in markets and supermarkets. Five hundred grams, or half a kilo, is a common quantity to order, and that converts to just over a pound (17.65 ounces, to be precise).

I'd like...	**Jeg vil gjerne ha...**	*yay vihl yar`•nuh hah...*
a (half) kilo of...	**en (halv) kilo...**	*ehn (hahl) khee´•lu...*
a (half) liter of...	**en (halv) liter...**	*ehn (hahl) lee´•tuhr...*
a piece of...	**et stykke...**	*eht stuik`•kuh...*
a slice of...	**en skive...**	*ehn shee`•vuh...*
More/Less than that.	**Mer/Mindre enn det.**	*mehr/mihn´•druh ehn deh*
How much?	**Hvor mye koster det?**	*voor mew`•uh kohs`•tuhr deh*
Where do I pay?	**Hvor betaler man?**	*voor buh•tah`•luhr mahn*
Can I have a bag?	**Kan jeg få en bærepose?**	*kahn yay faw ehn ba`•ruh•poo•suh*
I'm being helped.	**Jeg blir ekspedert.**	*yay bleer ehks•puh•deh´rt*

For Conversion Tables, see page 175.

YOU MAY HEAR...

Kan jeg hjelpe deg? *kahn yay yehl`•puh day*	Can I help you?
Hva skal det være? *vah skahl deh va`•ruh*	What would you like?
Skal det være noe annet? *skahl deh va`•ruh noo`•uh ahn`•nuht*	Anything else?
Det blir...kroner, takk. *deh bleer... kroo`n•uhr tahk*	That's...kroner, please.

In the Kitchen

bottle opener	**en flaskeåpner** ehn <u>flahs</u>`·kuh·**awp**·nuhr
bowls	**skåler** <u>skaw</u>`·luhr
can opener	**en boksåpner** ehn <u>bohks</u>`·**awp**·nuhr
cheese slicer	**ostehøvel** <u>us</u>`·tuh·hur·vuhl
corkscrew	**en korketrekker** ehn <u>kohr</u>`·kuh·trehk·kuhr
cups	**kopper** <u>kohp</u>`·puhr
forks	**gafler** <u>gahf</u>´·luhr
frying pan	**en stekepanne** ehn <u>steh</u>`·kuh·pahn·nuh
glasses	**glass** glahs
knives	**kniver** <u>kneev</u>`·uhr
measuring cup/	**et målebeger/en måleskje** eht <u>maw</u>`·luh·beh·guhr/
measuring spoon	ehn <u>maw</u>`·luh·sheh
napkins	**papirservietter** pah·<u>pee</u>´r·serv·yeht·tuhr
plates	**tallerkener** tah·<u>lehr</u>´·kuhn·uhr
pot	**en gryte** ehn <u>grui</u>`·tuh
saucepan	**en kasserolle** ehn kah·suh·<u>rohl</u>`·luh
spatula	**en slikkepott** ehn <u>slihk</u>`·kuh·poht
spoons	**skjeer** sheh`·uhrv

|

Drinks

ESSENTIAL

Can I have the wine list/drink menu?	**Kan jeg få se vinkartet/drikkekartet?** *kahn yay faw seh veen`-kahr-tuh/drihk`-kuh-kahr-tuh*
What do you recommend?	**Hva kan du anbefale?** *vah kahn dew ahn´-buh-fah-luh*
Can I have the house wine?	**Kan jeg få husets vin?** *kahn yay faw hew´s-uhs veen*
Can I buy you a drink?	**Kan jeg by på en drink?** *kahn yay bui poh ehn drihngk*
Cheers!	**Skål!** *skawl*
A coffee/tea, please.	**En kaffe/te, takk.** *ehn kahf´-fuh/teh tahk*
Black.	**Svart.** *svahrt*
With...	**Med...** *meh...*
milk	**melk** *mehlk*
sugar	**sukker** *suk´-kuhr*
artificial sweetener	**søtningsmiddel** *sur`t-nihngs-mihd-duhl*
A glass of..., please.	**Et glass..., takk.** *eht glahs...tahk*
juice	**juice** *yews*
soda	**soda** *soo´-dah*
(sparkling/still) water	**vann (med kullsyre/uten kullsyre)** *vahn (meh kewl`-sui-ruh/ew`-tuhn kewl`-sui-ruh)*
Is the tap water safe to drink?	**Kan man drikke vann rett fra springen?** *kahn mahn drihk`-kuh vahn reht frah sprihng´-uhn*

Non-alcoholic Drinks

ananasjuice *ahn´-nah-nahs-yews*	pineapple juice
appelsinjuice *ahp-puhl-see´n-yews*	orange juice
brus *brews*	soda

If you're not in the mood for Norwegian beer or spirits, there are a number of other drinks to enjoy. Tea and especially strong coffee are commonly drunk throughout the day. For soft drinks you could try **Solo** (orange-flavored soda) or **Mozell** (apple-flavored soda).

YOU MAY HEAR...

Hva vil du ha å drikke? *vah vihl dew hah aw drihk`·kuh*	What would you like to drink?
Med eller uten kullsyre? *meh ehl´·luhr ew`·tuhn kewl`·sui·ruh*	Sparkling or still water?

eplesaft *eh`·pluh·sahft*	apple juice
grapefruktjuice *grehp´·frewkt·yews*	grapefruit juice
iste *ee`s·teh*	iced tea
lettmelk *leht´·mehlk*	low-fat milk
melk *mehlk*	milk

mineralvann med kullsyre/uten kullsyre	sparkling/still mineral water
mih•nuh•**rahl**´•vahn meh _kewl_`•_sui_•ruh/	
_ew_`•tuhn _kewl_`•_sui_•ruh	
sitronbrus siht•_roo_´_n_•brews	lemonade

Aperitifs, Cocktails & Liqueurs

akevitt ah•kuh•_viht_´	aquavit
brandy _brehn_´-dih	brandy
gin tonic dshihn _tohn_´•nihk	gin and tonic
konjakk kohn•_yahk_´	cognac
likør lih•_kur_´r	liqueur
portvin _poort_´•veen	port
rom rum	rum
sherry _sher_´•rih	sherry
vermut _vehr_´•mewt	vermouth
vodka _vohd_´•kah	vodka
whisky _vihs_´•kih	whisky

Beer in Norway is classified by strength. **Lettøl** (beer with low
alcohol content) is less than 2.5% alcohol content and **zero** and
vørterøl are both non-alcoholic. **Pils** (lager) and **bayerøl** (medium-
strength dark beer) are relatively low in alcohol content. The strongest
beers (6-10%), like **eksportøl** (strong light beer) and **bokkøl** (strong
dark beer), are only sold at the **Vinmonopolet** (state-run liquor store).
If you are in Norway around Christmas time, be sure to try some of the
special limited-edition Christmas brews which are extremely popular
with the locals.
Beer, in addition to being drunk on its own, often serves as a chaser to
akevitt (aquavit), an extremely potent drink distilled from potato and
caraway seeds.

Beer

fatøl _fah`t·url_	draft [draught] beer
flaskeøl _flahs`·kuh·url_	bottled beer
lyst/mørkt øl _luist/murrkt url_	light/dark beer
pils _pihls_	lager
utenlandsk øl _ew`·tuhn·lahnsk url_	imported beer

Wine

avkjølt _ah´v·khurlt_	chilled
champagne _shahm·pahn´·yuh_	champagne
fyldig _fuil`·dih_	full-bodied
hvitvin _veet´·veen_	white
meget tørr _meh`·guht turr_	very dry
musserende _mews·seh´·ruh·nuh_	sparkling
rødvin _rur´·veen_	red
rosévin _roo·seh´·veen_	rosé
søt _surt_	sweet

On the Menu

abbor _ahb`·bohr_	perch
agurk _ah·gewr´k_	cucumber
akevitt _ah·kuh·viht´_	aquavit
akkar _ahk`·kahr_	squid
and _ahn_	duck
ananas _ahn´·nah·nahs_	pineapple
ananasjuice _ahn´·nah·nahs·yews_	pineapple juice
anisfrø _ah´·nihs·frur_	aniseed
ansjos _ahn·shoo´s_	anchovies or marinated sprats
appelsin _ahp·puhl·see´n_	orange
appelsinjuice _ahp·puhl·see´n·yews_	orange juice
appelsinmarmelade	orange marmalade
ahp·puhl·see´n·mahr·muh·lah·duh	
aprikos _ahp·rih·koo´s_	apricot
artisjokker _ar·tih·shohk´·kuhr_	artichokes
asparges _ahs·pahr´·guhs_	asparagus
aspargessuppe _ahs·pahr´·guhs·sewp·puh_	asparagus soup
aubergine _aw·buhr·shee´n_	eggplant [aubergine]
bacon _bay´·kuhn_	bacon
banan _bah·nah´n_	banana
basilikum _bah·see´·lih·kewm_	basil
benløse fugler _beh`n·lurs·uh few`l·uhr_	fried, rolled and stuffed slices of veal or beef
betasuppe _beh`·tah·sewp·puh_	thick meat and vegetable soup
biff _bihf_	beef steak
bjørnebær _byur`r·nuh·bar_	blackberries
blomkål _blohm´·kawl_	cauliflower
blomkålsuppe _blohm´·kawl·sewp·puh_	cauliflower soup

bløtkake _blur`t_•_kah_•kuh	layer cake
blåbær _blaw`_•bar	blueberries
blåskjell _blaw`_•shehl	mussels
blekksprut _blehk`_•sprewt	octopus
brandy _brehn´_-dih	brandy
brasme _brahs`_-muh	bream
brekkbønner _brehk´_-burn•nuhr	French beans
bringebær _brihng´_-uh•bar	raspberries
broiler _broi´_-luhr	chicken
brokkoli _brohk´_-koh•lih	broccoli
brisling _brihs`_-lihng	sprat, brisling
brun lapskaus brewn _lahps´_-kevs	Norwegian stew in brown gravy
brus brews	soda
brød brur	bread
buljong bewl•_yohng´_	consommé
bønner _burn`_-nuhr	beans
dadler _dahd´_-luhr	dates
dill dihl	dill
druer _drew`_-uhr	grapes
dyrestek _dui´_-ruh•stehk	roast venison

egg *ehg* — eggs

eggerøre *ehg`·guh·rur·ruh* — scrambled eggs

einebær *ay`·nuh·bar* — juniper berries

ekte geitost *ehk`·tuh yayt`·ust* — goat cheese

elg *ehlg* — moose

elgbiff *ehlg`·bihf* — moose steak

elgfilet *ehlg`·fih·leh* — fillet of moose

elgstek *ehlg`·stehk* — roast moose

eple *ehp`·luh* — apple

eplekake *ehp`·luh·kah·kuh* — apple pie

eplesaft *eh`·pluh·sahft* — apple juice

erter *ehr´·tuhr* — peas

fasan *fah·sah´n* — pheasant

fatøl *fah`t·url* — draft [draught] beer

fenalår *feh`·nah·lawr* — cured leg of mutton

fersken *fehrs´·kuhn* — peach

fikener *fee`·kuhn·uhr* — figs

fisk *fihsk* — fish

fiskeboller *fihs`·kuh·bohl·luhr* — fish balls

fiskekabaret *fihs`·kuh·kah·bah·reh* — assorted seafood and vegetables in aspic

fiskepudding *fihs`·kuh·pewd·dihng* — fish pudding

fiskesuppe *fihs`·kuh·sewp·puh* — fish soup

flyndre *fluin`·druh* — flounder

fløtemysost *flur´·tuh·muis·ust* — mild and sweet cow's milk cheese

fransk løksuppe *frahnsk lur`k·sewp·puh* — French onion soup

frokostblanding *froo´·kohst·blahn·nihng* — cereal

fruktkompott *frewkt´·kohm·poht* — stewed fruit

fårekjøtt *faw`·ruh·khurt* — mutton

fårestek *faw`·ruh·stehk* — roast leg of mutton or lamb

fårikål _faw´·rih·kawl_	mutton or lamb in cabbage stew
gammelost _gahm`·muhl·ust_	pungent cheese made with skimmed milk
gin tonic _dshihn tohn´·nihk_	gin and tonic
gjedde _yehd`·duh_	pike
grapefrukt _grehp´·frewkt_	grapefruit
grapefruktjuice _grehp´·frewkt·yews_	grapefruit juice
gravlaks _grah`v·lahks_	cured salmon flavored with dill
gresskar _grehs`·kahr_	pumpkin
gressløk _grehs`·lurk_	chives
grønnkål _grurn´·kawl_	kale
grønnsaksuppe _grurn`·sahk·sewp·puh_	vegetable soup
gudbrandsdalsost _gewd`·brahns·dahls·ust_	cow and goat's milk cheese
gul ertesuppe _gewl er`·tuh·sewp·puh_	yellow pea soup
gulrøtter _gew`l·rurt·tuhr_	carrots
gås _gaws_	goose
gåselever _gaw`·suh·leh·vuhr_	goose liver
hare _hah`·ruh_	hare
harestek _hah´·ruh·stehk_	roast hare
hasselnøtter _hahs´·suhl·nurt·tuhr_	hazelnuts
havregrøt _hahv`·ruh·grurt_	porridge
hellefisk _hehl`·luh·fihsk_	halibut
hjort _yohrt_	deer
hjortesadel _yohr`·tuh·sah·duhl_	saddle of deer
hodesalat _hoo´·duh·sah·laht_	lettuce
hoffdessert _hohf´·dehs·sar_	layers of meringue and whipped cream, topped with chocolate sauce and toasted almonds

honning _hohn`_·nihng	honey
hummer _hum´_·muhr	lobster
hvalbiff _vahl`_·bihf	whale steak
hvitløk _vee´t_·lurk	garlic
hvitting _viht`_·tihng	whiting
hvitvin _veet`_·veen	white wine
hyse _hui`_·suh	haddock (western Norway)
høne _hur`_·nuh	hen
ingefær _ihng´_·uh·far	ginger
is _ee_s	ice cream
iste _ee`s_·teh	iced tea
jarlsbergost _yahrls´_·behrg·ust	mild, slightly sweet, semi-hard cheese
jordbær _yoor´_·bar	strawberries
juice _yew_s	fruit juice
kaffe _kahf´_·fuh	coffee
kalkun kahl·_kew´n_	turkey
kalvebrissel _kahl`_·vuh·brihs·suhl	calf's sweetbread
kalvekjøtt _kahl`_·vuh·khurt	veal
kalvemedaljonger _kahl`_·vuh·meh·dahl·yohng·uhr	small round fillet of veal

kalvelever _kahl`·vuh·lehv·vuhr_	calf's liver
kamskjell _kahm`·shel_	scallop
kanel _kah·neh´l_	cinnamon
kanin _kah·nee´n_	rabbit
kapers _kah´·puhrs_	capers
karbonade _kahr·bu·nah`·duh_	hamburger
karpe _kahr`·puh_	carp
kastanjer _kahs·tahn´·yuhr_	chestnuts
karri _kahr´·rih_	curry seasoning
karve _kahr`·vuh_	caraway seeds
kaviar _kah·vih·ah´r_	caviar
kirsebær _khihr´·suh·bær_	cherries
kjøttboller _khurt`·bohl·uhr_	meatballs
kjøttkaker _khurt`·kahk·uhr_	small hamburgers
kjøttpudding _khurt`·pud·dihng_	meatloaf
kjøttsuppe _khurt`·sewp·puh_	meat soup
klippfisk _klihp´·fihsk_	salted and dried cod
knoke _knoo`·kuh_	bone
kokosnøtt _kuk´·kus·nurt_	coconut
kolje _kohl`·yuh_	haddock (eastern Norway)
korinter _ku·rihn´·tuhr_	currants
kotelett _koh·tuh·leht´_	chop
krabbe _krahb`·buh_	crab
kreps _krehps_	freshwater crayfish
kveite _kvay`·tuh_	halibut
kylling _khuil´·lihng_	chicken
kål _kawl_	cabbage
kålrabi/kålrot _kawl·rah´·bih/kawl´·root_	rutabaga [swede BE]
kantareller _kahn·tah·rehl´·luhr_	chanterelle mushrooms
karamellpudding _kah·rah·mehl´·pewd·dihng_	creme caramel
kokte poteter _kuk`·tuh pu·teh´t·uhr_	boiled potatoes

komler/komper _kum`_·luhr/_kum`_·puhr — potato dumplings (western Norway)

konjakk _kohn_·_yahk´_ — cognac
krem _krehm_ — whipped cream
laks _lahks_ — salmon
lammebog _lahm`_·muh·_boog_ — shoulder of lamb
lammebryst _lahm`_·muh·_bruist_ — brisket of lamb
lammekjøtt _lahm`_·muh·_khurt_ — lamb
lammelår _lahm`_·muh·_lawr_ — leg of lamb
lammesadel _lahm`_·muh·_sah_·duhl — saddle of lamb
lammestek _lahm`_·muh·st_ehk_ — roast lamb
lapskaus _lahps´_·kevs — Norwegian stew with meat, potatoes and vegetables

lettmelk _leht`_·mehlk — low-fat milk
lever _lehv´_·vuhr — liver
likør lih·_kur´r_ — liqueur
linser _lihn`_·suhr — lentils
lungemos _lung`_·uh·_moos_ — ground [minced] lungs and onions

lutefisk _lew`_·tuh·_fihsk_ — stockfish soaked in lye
lys lapskaus _luis_ _lahps´_·kevs — Norwegian stew with diced, salted and boiled pork

løk _lurk_ — onions
løksuppe _lur`k_·sewp·puh — onion soup
mais _mies_ — corn
maiskolbe _mies´_·kohl·buh — corn on the cob
mandarin mahn·dah·_ree´n_ — tangerine
mandelkake _mahn´_·duhl·k_ah_·kuh — almond cake
mandler _mahn´d_·luhr — almonds
makrell mahk·_rehl´_ — mackerel
markjordbær _mahr`k_·_yoor_·bar — wild strawberries

medisterkaker *meh·dihs´·tuhr·kah·kuhr*		small pork and beef hamburgers
medisterpølse *meh·dihs´·tuhr·purl·suh*		pork and beef sausage
melk *mehlk*		milk
melon *meh·loo´n*		melon
milkshake *mihlk´·shayk*		milkshake
mineralvann *mih·nuh·rahl´·vahn*		mineral water
molter/multer *mohl´·tuhr/mewl´·tuhr*		arctic cloudberries
moreller *mu·rehl´·luhr*		morello cherries
mørbradstek *mur´r·brahd·stehk*		roast sirloin
nektarin *nehk·tah·ree´n*		nectarine
nellik *nehl´·lihk*		clove
neslesuppe *nehs`·luh·sewp·puh*		nettle soup
nepe *neh`·puh*		turnip
normannaost *noor·mahn´·nah·ust*		blue-veined cow's milk cheese
nudler *newd´·luhr*		noodles
nypoteter *nui`·pu·teht·uhr*		new potatoes
nyrer *nui`·ruhr*		kidneys
nøtter *nurt´·tuhr*		nuts
oksebryst *ohk`·suh·bruist*		brisket of beef
oksefilet *ohk`·suh·fih·leh*		fillet of beef

oksehalesuppe <u>*ohk*</u>`·*suh*·*hah*·*luh*·*sewp*·*puh*	oxtail soup
oksekam <u>*ohk*</u>`·*suh*·*kahm*	loin
oksekjøtt <u>*ohk*</u>`·*suh*·*khurt*	beef
okserulader <u>*ohk*</u>`·*suh*·*rewl*·*lah*·*duhr*	braised beef rolls
oksestek <u>*ohk*</u>`·*suh*·*stehk*	roast beef
omelett *oh*·*muh*·<u>*leht*</u>´	omelet
orrfugl <u>*ohr*</u>`·*fewl*	black grouse, a woodland bird
ost *ust*	cheese
pannekaker <u>*pahn*</u>`·*nuh*·*kah*·*kuhr*	pancakes
paprika <u>*pahp*</u>´·*rih*·*kah*	sweet pepper
peanøtter <u>*pee*</u>´·*ah*·*nurt*·*tuhr*	peanuts
pepper <u>*pehp*</u>`·*puhr*	pepper
persille *pehr*·<u>*sihl*</u>`·*luh*	parsley
piggvar <u>*pihg*</u>`·*vahr*	turbot
pils *pihls*	lager
pinnekjøtt <u>*pihn*</u>`·*nuh*·*khurt*	salted and dried mutton ribs steamed on twigs
plommer <u>*plum*</u>`·*muhr*	plums
pommes frites *pohm friht*	French fries [chips]
portvin <u>*poort*</u>´·*veen*	port wine
potet *pu*·<u>*teh*</u>´*t*	potato

potetgull _pu·teh´t·gewl_	potato chips [crisps]
potetkroketter _pu·teh´t·krohk·keht·tuhr_	potato croquettes
potetmos _pu·teh´t·moos_	mashed potatoes
potetsalat _pu·teh´t·sah·laht_	potato salad
purre _pewr`·ruh_	leeks
pølse _purl`·suh_	sausage
pære _pa`·ruh_	pear
pære Belle Helene _pa`·ruh behl heh·leh`n_	poached pears with vanilla ice cream and chocolate
rabarbra _rah·bahr´·brah_	rhubarb
rakørret _rah`k·urr·ruht_	salt-cured and fermented trout
raspeball _rahs`·puh·bahl_	potato dumplings
reddiker _rehd´·dihk·kuhr_	radishes
regnbueørret _rayn`·bew·uh·urr·ruht_	rainbow trout
rekecocktail _reh`·kuh·kohk·tayl_	shrimp [prawn] cocktail
reker _reh`·kuhr_	shrimp [prawns]
rips _rihps_	red currants
ris _rees_	rice
ristet brød _rihs`·tuht brur_	toast
rogn _rohngn_	roe
rognebær _rohng`·nuh·bar_	rowanberries
rosenkål _roo´·suhn·kawl_	Brussels sprouts
rosiner _ru·see´·nuhr_	raisins
rundstykke _rewn´·stuik·kuh_	roll
rødbeter _rur`·beh·tuhr_	beet [beetroot]
rødkål _rur´·kawl_	red cabbage
rødspette _rur`·speht·tuh_	plaice
røkelaks _rur`·kuh·lahks_	smoked salmon
røye _rury`·uh_	char
rådyr _raw´·duir_	roe-deer

rådyrsadel _raw´·duir·sah·duhl_ — saddle of venison

rådyrstek _raw´·duir·stehk_ — roast venison

ragu _rah·gew´_ — ragout

rapphøne _rahp`·hur·nuh_ — partridge

reinsdyr _rayns´·duir_ — reindeer

reinsdyrmedaljonger _rayns´·duir·meh·dahl·yohng·uhr_ — small, round fillets of reindeer

reinsdyrstek _rayns´·duir·stehk_ — roast reindeer

ribbe _rihb`·buh_ — spareribs

ridderost _rihd´·duhr·ust_ — semi-hard cheese with nutty flavor

riskrem _ree´s·krehm_ — creamed rice with red berry sauce

roastbiff _rohst´·bihf_ — broiled steak

rom _rum_ — rum

rosévin _roo·seh´·veen_ — rosé wine

rype _rui´·puh_ — grouse, a mountain bird

rødgrøt med fløte _rur`·grurt meh flur`·tuh_ — berry compote with cream

rødvin _rur´·veen_ — red wine

salat _sah·lah´t_ — salad

salt _sahlt_ — salt

saltkjøttlapskaus _sahlt`•khurt•lahps´•kevs_	Norwegian stew with diced, salted and boiled pork
salvie _sahl•vee`•uh_	sage
sardell _sar•dehl´_	canned anchovy
sardin _sar•dee´n_	sardine
sei _say_	pollock
selleri _sehl•luhr•ee´_	celery
sellerisuppe _seh•luh•ree´•sewp•puh_	celery soup
sherry _sher´•rih_	sherry
sik _seek_	whitefish
sild _sihl_	herring
sildeball _sihl`•luh•bahl_	potato dumplings filled with minced salted herring
sitron _siht•roo´n_	lemon
sitronbrus _siht•roo´n•brews_	lemonade
sjampinjonger _sham•pihn•yohng´•uhr_	button mushrooms
sjampinjongsuppe _shahm•pihn•yohng´•sewp•puh_	button mushroom soup
sjokoladepudding _shu•ku•lah`•duh•pewd•dihng_	chocolate pudding
sjømat _shur`•maht_	seafood
sjøørret _shur`•urr•ruht_	sea trout
sjøtunge _shur`•tung•uh_	sole
skalldyr _skahl`•duir_	shellfish
skinke _shihng`•kuh_	ham
slettvar _sleht`•vahr_	brill
smør _smurr_	butter
solbær _soo´l•bar_	black currants
sopp _sohp_	mushrooms
sorbett _sohr•beht´_	sorbet
spinat _spih•nah´t_	spinach

steinbit _stayn`•beet_	catfish
stek _stehk_	roast
stekte poteter _stehk`•tuh pu•teh´t•uhr_	sautéed potatoes
stikkelsbær _stihk´•kuhls•bar_	gooseberries
stuede poteter _stew`•eh•duh pu•teh´t•uhr_	potatoes in a white sauce
stør _sturr_	sturgeon
størje _sturr`•yuh_	tuna
soufflé _sewf•leh´_	soufflé
surkål _sew´r•kawl_	coleslaw
sursild _sew´r•sihl_	marinated herring
svinefilet _svee`•nuh•fih•leh_	fillet of pork
svinekam _svee`•nuh•kahm_	loin of pork
svinekjøtt _svee`•nuh•khurt_	pork
svinestek _svee`•nuh•stehk_	roast pork
svisker _svihs`•kuhr_	prunes
svor _svoor_	bacon rind [crackling]
sylte _suil`•tuh_	head cheese [brawn]
sylteagurk _suil`•tuh•ah•gewrk_	pickled gherkin
syltetøy _suil`•tuh•tury_	jam
tartarbiff _tahr•tah´r•bihf_	steak tartare
T-benstek _teh´•behn•stehk_	T-bone steak
te _teh_	tea
terte _tehr´•tuh_	fruit cake
tilslørte bondepiker _tihl´•slurr•tuh bun´•nuh•pee•kuhr_	layers of stewed apples, cookie [biscuit] crumbs and whipped cream
timian _tee´•mih•ahn_	thyme
tomater _tu•maht´•uhr_	tomatoes
tomatsuppe _tu•mah´t•sewp•puh_	tomato soup
torsk _tohrsk_	cod
tranebær _trah`•nuh•bar_	cranberries
tunfisk _tew`n•fihsk_	tuna

tunge _tung`·uh_	tongue
tyttebær _tuit´·tuh·bar_	lingonberry
tørrfisk _turr´·fihsk_	stockfish
uer _ew`·uhr_	rosefish (seafood)
vafler _vahf´·luhr_	waffles
vaktel _vahk´·tuhl_	quail
valnøtter _vahl´·nurt·tuhr_	walnuts
vaniljesaus _vah·nihl`·yuh·sevs_	vanilla sauce
vannmelon _vahn`·meh·loon_	watermelon
varm sjokolade _vahrm shu·ku·lah`·duh_	hot chocolate
vermut _vehr´·mewt_	vermouth
villand _vihl`·lahn_	wild duck
vin _veen_	wine
vodka _vohd´·kah_	vodka
whisky _vihs´·kih_	whisky
wienerschnitzel _vee´·nuhr·shniht·suhl_	breaded veal cutlet
yoghurt _yoo´·gewrt_	yogurt
øl _url_	beer
ørret _urr`·ruht_	trout
østers _urs´·tehrs_	oysters
åbor _aw`·bohr_	perch
ål _awl_	eel

People

ESSENTIAL

Hello/Hi!	**Hallo/Hei!** *hah·loo ́/hay*
How are you?	**Hvordan står det til?** *voor ́·dahn stawr deh tihl*
Fine, thanks.	**Bare bra, takk.** *bah`·ruh brah tahk*
Excuse me.	**Unnskyld.** *ewn ́·shewl*
Do you speak English?	**Snakker du engelsk?** *snahk`·kuhr dew ehng ́·ehlsk*
What's your name?	**Hva heter du?** *vah heh`·tuhr dew*
My name is...	**Jeg heter...** *yay heh`·tuhr...*
Nice to meet you!	**Hyggelig å treffes!** *huig`·guh·lih aw trehf ́·fuhs*
Where are you from?	**Hvor kommer du fra?** *voor kohm`·muhr dew frah*
I'm from the U.S./	**Jeg er fra USA/Storbritannia.** *yay ar frah*
the U.K.	*ew·ehs·ah ́/stoo ́r·brih·tahn·yah*
What do you do?	**Hva jobber du med?** *vah yohb`·buhr dew meh*
I work for...	**Jeg jobber for...** *yay yohb`·buhr fohr...*
I'm a student.	**Jeg er student.** *yay ar stew·dehnt ́*
I'm retired.	**Jeg er pensjonist.** *yay ar pang·shu·nihst ́*
Do you like...?	**Liker du...?** *lee ́·kuhr dew...*
Goodbye.	**Adjø.** *ahd·yur ́*
See you later.	**Vi ses.** *vee seh`·uhs*

Language Difficulties

Do you speak English?	**Snakker du engelsk?** *snahk`·kuhr dew ehng ́·uhlsk*
Does anyone here speak English?	**Er det noen her som snakker engelsk?** *ar deh noo`·uhn har sohm snahk`·kuhr ehng ́·uhlsk*
I don't speak (much) Norwegian.	**Jeg snakker ikke (så bra) norsk.** *yay snahk`·kuhr ihk`·kuh (saw brah) norsk*

De (the formal form of 'you') is generally no longer used to address strangers, but is restricted to written works and addressing older people. As a general rule, **du** can be used in all situations without offending anyone.

Could you speak more slowly?	**Kan du snakke litt langsommere?** *kahn dew snahk`•kuh liht lahng`•sohm•muh•ruh*
Could you repeat that?	**Kan du gjenta det?** *kahn dew yehn´•tah deh*
Excuse me.	**Unnskyld.** *ewn´•shewl*
What was that?	**Hva sa du?** *vah sah dew*
Can you write it down?	**Kan du skrive det?** *kahn dew skree`•vuh deh*
Can you translate this for me?	**Kan du oversette dette for meg?** *kahn dew aw`•vuhr•seht•tuh deht`•tuh fohr may*
What does this mean?	**Hva betyr dette?** *vah buh•tui´r deht`•tuh*
I (don't) understand.	**Jeg forstår (ikke).** *yay for•staw´r (ihk`•kuh)*
Do you understand?	**Forstår du?** *for•staw´r dew*

YOU MAY HEAR...

Jeg snakker ikke engelsk.
yay snahk`•kuhr ihk`•kuh ehng´•uhlsk

I don't speak English.

Jeg snakker bare litt engelsk. _yay
sahk•ehr bahr•eh liht ehn•gehlsk_

I only speak a little
English.

Making Friends

Hello/Hi!	**Hallo/Hei!** _hah•loo´/hay_	
Good morning.	**God morgen.** _gum•maw`•ruhn_	
Good afternoon.	**God dag.** _gud•dah´g_	
Good evening.	**God aften/God kveld.** _gu•ahf´•tuhn/guk•kvehl´_	
My name is...	**Jeg heter...** _yay heh´•tuhr..._	
Can I introduce you to...?	**Kan jeg få presentere deg for...?** _kahn yay faw pre•sahng•teh´•ruh day fohr..._	
Nice to meet you!	**Hyggelig å treffes!** _huig´•guh•lih oh trehf`•fuhs_	
How are you?	**Hvordan står det til?** _voor´•dahn stawr deh tihl_	
Fine, thanks.	**Bare bra, takk.** _bah`•ruh brah tahk_	
And you?	**Og med deg?** _oh meh day_	

Travel Talk

I'm here...	**Jeg er her...** _yay ar har..._	
on business	**i forretninger** _ih fohr•reht´•nihng•uhr_	
on vacation [holiday]	**på ferie** _poh feh´r•yuh_	
studying	**som student** _sohm stew•dehn´t_	
I'm staying for...	**Jeg blir her...** _yay bleer har..._	
I've been here...	**Jeg har vært her...** _yay hahr vehrt har..._	
a day	**en dag** _ehn dahg_	
a week	**en uke** _ehn ew`•kuh_	
a month	**en måned** _ehn maw`•nuhd_	

Where are you from?	**Hvor kommer du fra?** *voor <u>kohm´</u>-muhr d**ew** frah*
I'm from…	**Jeg er fra…** *yay* **ar** *frah…*

For Numbers, see page 170.

Personal

Who are you with?	**Hvem reiser du sammen med?** *vehm <u>ray´</u>-suhr d**ew** <u>sahm´</u>-muhn meh*
I'm on my own.	**Jeg reiser alene.** *yay <u>ray´</u>-suhr ah-<u>leh´</u>-nuh*
I'm with…	**Jeg er her med…** *yay ar har meh…*
my husband/wife	**mannen min/kona mi** *<u>mahn´</u>-nuhn mihn/<u>koo´</u>-nah mih*
my boyfriend/ girlfriend	**kjæresten min** *<u>kha´</u>-reh-stuhn mihn*
a friend	**en venn** *ehn vehn*
a colleague	**en kollega** *ehn kohl-<u>leh´</u>-gah*
colleagues	**kolleger** *kul•ehg•ehr*
When's your birthday?	**Når har du bursdag?** *nohr <u>hahr</u> dew <u>bew´</u>rs-dahg*
How old are you?	**Hvor gammel er du?** *voor <u>gahm´</u>-muhl ar d**ew***
I'm…	**Jeg er…** *yay* **ar**…
Are you married?	**Er du gift?** *ar dew yihft*
I'm…	**Jeg er…** *yay ar…*
single	**ugift** *<u>ew´</u>•yihft*
in a relationship	**opptatt** *<u>ohp´</u>•taht*
engaged	**Jeg er forlovet** *yay ar fawr•lawv•eht*
married	**gift** *yihft*
divorced	**skilt** *shihlt*
separated	**separert** *seh•pah•<u>reh´</u>rt*
I'm widowed.	**Jeg er enkemann m /enke f.** *yay ar <u>ehng´</u>•kuh•mahn/<u>ehng´</u>•kuh*

Do you have children/ grandchildren?	**Har du barn/barnebarn?** _hahr_ d**ew** b**ah**rn/ _bah`rn•uh•b**ah**rn_

For Numbers, see page 170.

Work & School

What do you do?	**Hva jobber du med?** vah _yohb`•buhr_ d**ew** meh
What are you studying?	**Hva studerer du?** vah stew•_deh´•ruhr_ d**ew**
I'm studying...	**Jeg studerer...** yay stew•_deh´•ruhr..._
I work full time/ part time.	**Jeg jobber fulltid/deltid.** yay _yohb`•bur fewl´•teed/ dehl´•teed_
I am unemployed.	**Jeg er arbeidsledig.** yay ar ahr•bayds•leh•dihg
I work at home.	**Jeg jobber hjemmefra.** yay jawb•ehr yem•eh•frah
Who do you work for?	**Hvem jobber du for?** vehm _yohb`•buhr_ d**ew** fohr
I work for...	**Jeg jobber for...** yay _yohb`•buhr_ fohr...
Here's my business card.	**Her er visittkortet mitt.** har ar vihs•_iht´•_kor•tuh miht

For Business Travel, see page 144.

Weather

What's the weather forecast?	**Hva sier værmeldingen?** *vah see`·uhr var`·mehl·lihng·uhn*
What beautiful weather!	**Så fint vær det er!** *soh feent var deh ar*
What terrible weather!	**For et forferdelig vær!** *fohr eht fohr·fehr´·duh·lih var*
It's cool/warm.	**Det er kjølig/varmt.** *deh ar khur`·lih/vahrmt*
It's snowy/icy.	**Det snør/er kaldt.** *deh snurr/ar kahlt*
It's rainy.	**Det regner.** *deh rayn`·uhr*
It's sunny.	**Sola skinner.** *soo´·lah shih´·nuhr*
Do I need a jacket/ an umbrella?	**Trenger jeg jakke/paraply?** *trehng´·uhr yay yahk`·kuh/pah·rah·plui´*

For Temperature, see page 176.

ESSENTIAL

Would you like to go out for a drink/meal?	**Skal vi gå og ta en drink/ut og spise?** *skahl vee gaw oh tah ehn dringk/ewt oh <u>spee</u>`·suh*
What are your plans for tonight/tomorrow?	**Hva gjør du i kveld/i morgen?** *vah yurr dew ih kvehl/ih <u>maw</u>`·ruhn*
Can I have your number?	**Kan jeg få nummeret ditt?** *kahn yay faw <u>num</u>´·muhr·uh diht*
Can I join you?	**Er det opptatt her?** *ar deh awp·that har*
Can I buy you a drink?	**Kan jeg by på en drink?** *kahn yay bui poh ehn drihngk*
I like you.	**Jeg liker deg.** *yay <u>lee</u>´·kuhr day*
I love you.	**Jeg elsker deg.** *yay <u>ehls</u>`·kuhr day*

The Dating Game

Would you like to go out for coffee?	**Skal vi gå og ta en kaffe?** *skahl vee gaw oh tah ehn <u>kahf</u>´·fuh*
Would you like to go out for a drink/ for dinner?	**Har du lyst å ta en drink/gå og spise middag?** *hahr dew lyst aw tah ehn drihnk/gaw awg spih·seh mihd·ahg*
What are your plans for...?	**Hva gjør du...?** *vah yurr dew...*
tonight	**i kveld** *ih kvehl*
tomorrow	**i morgen** *ih <u>maw</u>`·ruhn*
this weekend	**i helgen** *ih <u>hehl</u>´·guhn*
Where would you like to go?	**Hvor vil du dra?** *voor vihl dew drah*
I'd like to go to...	**Jeg vil gjerne dra til...** *yay vihl <u>ya</u>`r·nuh drah tihl...*

Do you like…?	**Liker du…?** _lee´-kuhr dew_…	
Can I have your number/e–mail?	**Kan jeg få nummeret ditt/e-postadressen din?** _kahn yay faw num´-muh-ruh diht/ eh´-pohst-ahd-rehs-suhn dihn_	
Are you on Facebook/Twitter?	**Er du på Facebook/Twitter?** _Ar dew paw feis-bewk/ tviht-ehr_	
Can I join you?	**Kan jeg slå meg ned her?** _kahn yay slaw may nehd har_	
You're very attractive.	**Du er svært tiltrekkende.** _dew ar svart tihl´-trehk-kuhn-uh_	
Should we go somewhere quieter?	**Skal vi gå til et roligere sted?** _skahl vee gaw tihl eht roo´-lih-uh-ruh stehd_	

For Communications, see page 49.

Accepting & Rejecting

I'd love to, thanks.	**Takk, det vil jeg gjerne.** _tahk deh vihl yay ya`r-nuh_	
Where should we meet?	**Hvor skal vi møtes?** _voor skahl vee mur´-tuhs_	
Let's meet at the bar/your hotel.	**Vi møtes i baren/på hotellet ditt.** _vee mur´-tuhs ee bah´-ruhn/poh hu-tehl´-luh diht_	
I'll come by at…	**Jeg henter deg…** _yay hehn`-tuhr day_…	

What's your address?	**Hva er adressen din?** *vah ar ahd•rehs´•suhn dihn*
Thanks, but I'm busy.	**Takk, men jeg er dessverre opptatt.** *tahk mehn yay ar dehs•vehr´•ruh ohp´•taht*
I'm not interested.	**Jeg er ikke interessert.** *yay ar ihk`•kuh ihn•truhs•seh´rt*
Leave me alone.	**Vær så snill å la meg være i fred.** *var soh snihl oh lah may va`•ruh ih freh*
Stop bothering me!	**Slutt å plage meg!** *slewt oh plah`•guh may*

For Time, see page 171.

Getting Intimate

Can I hug/kiss you?	**Kan jeg holde rundt/kysse deg?** *kahn yay hohl´•luh rewnt/khuis`•suh day*
Yes.	**Ja.** *yah*
No.	**Nei.** *nay*
Stop!	**Stopp!** *stohp*
I love you.	**Jeg elsker deg.** *yay ehls`•kuhr day*

Sexual Preferences

Are you gay?	**Er du homofil?** *ar dew hu•mu•fee´l*
I'm...	**Jeg er...** *yay ar...*
heterosexual	**heterofil** *heh•teh•ru•fee´l*
homosexual	**homofil** *hu•mu•fee´l*
bisexual	**bifil** *bih•fee´l*
Do you like men/women?	**Liker du menn/kvinner?** *lee´•kuhr dew mehn/kvihn`•nuhr*

Leisure Time

Sightseeing

ESSENTIAL

Where's the tourist information office?	**Hvor er turistkontoret?** *voor ar tew-<u>rihst</u>´-kun-**too**-ruh*
What are the main points of interest?	**Hva er de viktigste severdighetene?** *vah <u>ar</u> dih <u>vihk</u>`-tik-stuh seh-<u>vehr</u>´-dih-heh-tuh-nuh*
Do you have tours in English?	**Har dere omvisninger på engelsk?** *hahr deh`-ruh <u>ohm</u>´-vihs-nihng-uhr poh <u>ehng</u>´-uhlsk*
Can I have a map/guide?	**Kan jeg få et kart/en guide?** *kahn yay faw eht kahrt/ehn gied*

Tourist Information

Do you have any information on…?	**Har dere informasjon om…?** *hahr deh`-ruh ihn-fohr-mah-<u>shoo</u>´n ohm…*
Can you recommend…?	**Kan dere anbefale…?** *kahn <u>deh</u>`-ruh <u>ahn</u>´-buh-**fah**-luh…*
a boat trip	**en båttur** *ehn <u>bawt</u>´-tewr*
an excursion	**en utflukt** *ehn <u>ew</u>`t-flewkt*
a sightseeing tour	**en sightseeingtur** *ehn <u>siet</u>´-see-ihng-tewr*

Tourist offices are located throughout Norway. The local tourist office can provide information for visitors on accommodation, activities and other entertainment. Visit Norway, the official website of the Norwegian Tourist Board, www.visitnorway.com, can provide information about locations in particular cities.

On Tour

I'd like to go on the tour to…	**Jeg vil gjerne bli med på turen til…** *yay vihl ya`r•nuh blih meh poh tew´•ruhn tihl…*
When's the next tour?	**Når går neste tur?** *nohr gawr nehs`•tuh tewr*
Are there tours in English?	**Fins det turer på engelsk?** *fihns deh tew´r•uhr poh ehng´•uhlsk*
Is there an English-speaking guide/an audio guide in English?	**Fins det en engelsktalende guide/en lydguide på engelsk?** *fihns deh ehn ehng´•uhlsk•tahl•uhn•uh gied/ehn luid`•gied poh ehng´•uhlsk*
What time do we leave?	**Når drar vi?** *nohr drahr vee*
What time do we return?	**Når kommer vi tilbake?** *nohr kohm´•muhr vee tihl•bah`•kuh*
We'd like to see…	**Vi vil gjerne se på…** *vee vihl ya`r•nuh seh poh…*
Can we stop here…?	**Kan vi stoppe her…?** *kahn vee stohp`•puh har…*
to take photographs	**for å ta bilder** *fohr oh tah bihl`•duhr*
to buy souvenirs	**for å kjøpe suvenirer** *fohr oh khur`•puh sew•vuh•nee´r•uhr*
to use the restroom [toilet]	**for å gå på toalettet** *forh oh gaw poh tu•ah•leh´•tuh*

Is it disabled-accessible? **Er det adkomst for bevegelseshemmede?** *ar deh ahd`·kohmst fohr buh·veh´·guhl·suhs·hem·muhd·uh*

For Tickets, see page 20.

Seeing the Sights

Where is/are...?	**Hvor er...?**	*voor ar...*
the battleground	**slagstedet**	*slah´g·steh·duh*
the botanical gardens	**den botaniske hagen**	*dehn bu·tah´·nihsk·uh hah`·guhn*
the castle	**slottet**	*slot´·tuh*
the downtown area	**sentrum**	*sehn´·trewm*
the fair	**markedet**	*mahr`·kehd·uh*
the fortress	**festningen**	*fehst`·nihng·uhn*
the fountain	**fontenen**	*fon·teh`·nuhn*
the library	**biblioteket**	*bihb·lyu·teh´·kuh*
the market	**torget**	*tohr´·guh*
the museum	**museet**	*mew·seh´·uh*
the old town	**gamlebyen**	*gahm`·luh·bui·uhn*
the palace	**slottet**	*slot´·tuh*
the park	**parken**	*pahr´·kuhn*

the ruins	**ruinene** _rew•**ee**´n•uh•nuh_
the shopping area	**handlestrøket** _hahn`d•luh•str**ur**•kuh_
the town square	**rådhusplassen** _r**aw**d`•h**ew**s•pl**ah**•suhn_
Can you show me on the map?	**Kan du vise meg på kartet hvor jeg er?** _kahn d**ew** v**ee**´•suh may paw k**ahr**´•tuh voor yay ar_
It's…	**Det er…** _deh ar…_
amazing	**praktfullt** _pr**ahk**t`•fewlt_
beautiful	**vakkert** _v**ah**k´•kuhrt_
boring	**kjedelig** _kh**eh**`•duh•lih_
interesting	**interessant** _ihn•tuh•rehs•s**ahng**´t_
magnificent	**storslagent** _st**oo**`r•sl**ah**g•uhnt_
romantic	**romantisk** _ru•m**ahn**´•tihsk_
strange	**underlig** _**ewn**`•dur•lih_
stunning	**overveldende** _**aw**`•vuhr•vehl•duhn•uh_
terrible	**forferdelig** _fohr•f**a**´r•duh•lih_
ugly	**stygt** _stuikt_
I (don't) like it.	**Jeg liker det (ikke).** _yay l**ee**´•kuhr deh (**ihk**`•kuh)_

For Asking Directions, see page 34.

Religious Sites

Where's...?	**Hvor er...?** *voor ar...*
the cathedral	**domkirken** _dohm´·khihr·kuhn_
the church	**kirken** _khihr`·kuhn_
the mosque	**moskéen** _mus·**keh**´·uhn_
the synagogue	**synagogen** _sui·nah·**goo**`·guhn_
the temple	**templet** _tehm´p·luh_
What time is mass/ the service?	**Når begynner messen/gudstjenesten?** *nohr buh·**yuin**´·nuhr mehs`·suhn/**gewds**´·ty**eh**·nuhs·tuhn*

Shopping

ESSENTIAL

Where is the market/ mall [shopping centre]?	**Hvor er torget/kjøpesenteret?** *voor ar tohr´·guh/ **khur**`·puh·sehn·truh*
I'm just looking.	**Jeg bare ser meg omkring.** *yay **bah**`·ruh sehr may ohm·**krihng**´*
Can you help me?	**Kan du hjelpe meg?** *kahn dew **yehl**`·puh may*
I'm being helped.	**Jeg får hjelp.** *yay fawr yehlp*
How much?	**Hvor mye koster det?** *voor **mew**`·uh **kohs**`·tuhr deh*
That one.	**Den der.** *dehn dar*
No, thanks. That's all.	**Nei takk. Det var alt.** *nay tahk deh **vahr** ahlt*
Where do I pay?	**Hvor betaler man?** *voor buh·**tah**´·luhr mahn*
I'll pay in cash/by credit card.	**Jeg betaler kontant/med kredittkort.** *yay buh·**tah**´·luhr kun·**tahn**´t/meh kreh·**diht**´·kohrt*
Could I have a receipt?	**Kan jeg få kvittering?** *kahn yay faw kviht·**teh**´·rihng*

YOU MAY SEE...

UTE TIL LUNSJ	closed for lunch
BETAL HER	pay here
VI TAR KREDITTKORT	credit cards accepted
ÅPNINGSTIDER	opening hours

At the Shops

Where is…?	**Hvor er det…?** *voor ar deh…*
the antiques store	**en antikvitetshandel** *ehn ahn·tih·kvih·<u>teh´ts</u>·hahn·duhl*
the bakery	**et bakeri** *eht bah·kuhr·<u>ee´</u>*
the bank	**en bank** *ehn bahngk*
the bookstore	**en bokhandel** *ehn <u>book</u>`·hahn·duhl*
the clothing store	**en klesbutikk** *ehn <u>kleh</u>`s·bew·tihk*
the delicatessen	**en delikatesseforretning** *ehn deh·lih·kah·<u>tehs´</u>·suh·fohr·reht·nihng*
the department store	**et stormagasin** *eht <u>stoor</u>`·mah·gah·seen*
the gift shop	**en gavebutikk** *ehn <u>gah</u>`·vuh·bew·tihk*

Norway offers shopping choices for a range of budgets. Even in the capital, a good deal of shopping can be done on foot. Many of the major stores are located in the area around **Karl Johans** gate and on **Bogstadveien** and **Hegdehaugsveien** streets. **Grünerløkka** is the place to go to find trendy boutiques showcasing the work of young Norwegian designers. Here you'll also find lots of second-hand shops, music stores and independent stores selling local pottery and handicrafts. For everything under one roof in Oslo, visit **Aker Brygge**, **Byporten**, **Glasmagasinet**, **Oslo City**, **Paleet**, **Steen & Strøm** and **Vikaterrassen**.

Regular store hours are Monday to Friday from 9:00 a.m. to 5:00 p.m. (on Saturday to 3:00 p.m.), but many stores stay open later. Shopping malls are generally open Monday to Friday from 10:00 a.m. to 9:00 p.m. and Saturday from 9:00 a.m. to 6:00 p.m. Most stores are closed on Sunday.

the health food store	**en helsekostbutikk** *ehn hehl`·suh·kohst·fohr·reht·nihng*	
the jeweler	**en gullsmed** *ehn gewl`·smeh*	
the liquor store [off-licence]	**et vinmonopol** *eht vee`n·mu·nu·pool*	
the market	**et torg** *eht tohrg*	
the music store	**musikkforretningen** *mews·ihk·fawr·eht·nihng·ehn*	
the pastry shop	**et konditori** *eht kun·dih·tu·ree´*	
the pharmacy [chemist]	**et apotek** *eht ah·pu·teh´k*	
the produce [grocery] store	**en matvarebutikk** *ehn mah`t·vah·ruh·bew·tihk*	
the shoe store	**en skoforretning** *ehn skoo´·fohr·reht´·nihng*	
the shopping mall	**et butikksenter** *eht bew·tihk´·sehn·tuhr*	
the souvenir store	**en suvenirbutikk** *ehn sew·vuh·nee´r·bew·tihk*	

YOU MAY HEAR...

Kan jeg hjelpe deg? *kahn yay yehl`·puh day*

Can I help you?

Et øyeblikk. *eht ury`·uh·blihk*

One moment.

Hva skal det være? *vah skahl deh va`·ruh*

What would you like?

Skal det være noe annet? *skahl deh va`·ruh noo`·uh ahn`·nuht*

Anything else?

Where is...?	**Hvor er det...?** *voor ar deh...*	
the supermarket	**et supermarked** *eht sew`·puhr·mahr·kuhd*	
the tobacconist	**en tobakksbutikk** *ehn tu·bahk`s·bew·tihk*	
the toy store	**en leketøysbutikk** *ehn leh`·kuh·turys·bew·tihk*	

Ask an Assistant

When do you open/close?	**Når åpner/stenger dere?** *nawr åwpn·er/stehng·ehr dehr·eh*	
When does... open/close?	**Når åpner/stenger...?** *nohr aw`p·nuhr/stehng`·uhr...*	
Where is...?	**Hvor er...?** *voor ar...*	
the cash desk	**kassen** *kahs`·suhn*	
the escalator	**rulletrappen** *rewl`·luh·trahp·puhn*	
the elevator [lift]	**heisen** *hay´·suhn*	
the fitting room	**prøverommet** *prur`·vuh·rum·muh*	
the store directory [guide]	**butikkguiden** *bew·tihk´·gie·duhn*	
Can you help me?	**Kan du hjelpe meg?** *kahn dew yehl`·puh may*	
I'm just looking.	**Jeg bare ser meg omkring.** *yay bah`·ruh sehr may ohm·krihng´*	
I'm being helped.	**Jeg får hjelp.** *yay fawr yehlp*	

Do you have anything in…?	**Har du noe i…?**	_hahr dew noo`-uh ih…_
Can you show me…?	**Kan du vise meg…?**	_kahn dew vee`-suh may…_
Can you ship/wrap it?	**Kan du sende den/pakke den inn?**	_kahn dew seh`-nuh dehn/pahk`-kuh dehn ihn_
How much?	**Hvor mye koster det?**	_voor mui`-uh kohs`-tuhr deh_
That's all.	**Det var alt.**	_deh var ahlt_

For Clothing, see page 124.

For Souvenirs, see page 130.

Personal Preferences

I'd like something…	**Jeg vil gjerne ha noe…**	_yay vihl ya`r-nuh hah noo`-uh…_
cheap/expensive	**billig/dyrt**	_bihl`-lih/duirt_
larger/smaller	**større/mindre**	_sturr´-ruh/mihn´-druh_
from this region	**fra dette området**	_frah deht`-tuh ohm`-raw-duh_
Is it real?	**Er den ekte?**	_ar dehn ehk`-tuh_
Could you show me this/that?	**Kan du vise meg den/den der?**	_kahn dew vee`-suh may dehn/dehn dar_
It's not quite what I want.	**Det var ikke akkurat det jeg hadde tenkt meg.**	_deh vahr ihk`-kuh ahk`-kew-raht deh yay hahd`-duh tehngkt may_

Major credit cards are accepted at most hotels, restaurants, large shops, car rental companies and airlines, though some places will not accept them, particularly supermarkets and gas stations. It is a good idea to have some cash on hand, just in case. Traveler's checks are a safe alternative to cash, especially if you do not have a credit card.

No, I don't like it.	**Nei, jeg liker det ikke.**	nay yay _lee´_•kuhr deh _ihk´_•kuh
That's too expensive.	**Det er for dyrt.**	deh ar fohr duirt
I'd like to think about it.	**Jeg må tenke på det.**	yay moh _tehng´_•kuh poh deh
I'll take it.	**Jeg tar det.**	yay tahr deh

Paying & Bargaining

How much?	**Hvor mye koster det?**	voor _mui´_•uh _kohs´_•tuhr deh
I'll pay...	**Jeg betaler...**	yay buh•_tah´_•luhr...
in cash	**kontant**	kun•_tahn´t_
by credit card	**med kredittkort**	meh kreh•_diht´_•kohrt
by traveler's check [cheque]	**med reisesjekk**	meh _ray´_•suh•shehk
Could I have a receipt?	**Kan jeg få kvittering?**	kahn yay faw kviht•_teh´_•rihng
That's too much.	**Det er for mye.**	deh ar fohr _mew´_•uh
I'll give you...	**Jeg gir deg...**	yay yeer day...
I only have...kroner.	**Jeg har bare...kroner.**	yay hahr _bah´_•ruh... _kroo´_•nuhr
Is that your best price?	**Er det ditt siste tilbud?**	ar deh diht _sihs´_•tuh _tihl´_•bewd
Can you give me a discount?	**Kan du gi meg avslag?**	kahn dew yee may _ahv´_•slahg

For Numbers, see page 170.

Making a Complaint

I'd like…	**Jeg vil gjerne…** *yay vihl ya`r·nuh…*
to exchange this	**bytte dette** *buit`·tuh deht`·tuh*
to return this	**levere dette tilbake** *leh·veh´·ruh deht`·tuh tihl·bah`·kuh*
a refund	**ha pengene tilbake** *hah pehng`·uh·nuh tihl· bah`·kuh*
to see the manager	**snakke med butikksjefen** *snahk`·kuh meh buw·tihk´·shehf·uhn*

YOU MAY HEAR…

Hvordan vil du betale? *voor´·dahn vihl dew buh·tah´·luh*	How are you paying?
Kredittkortet ditt ble avslått. *kreh·diht·kurt·eht diht bleh ahv·slawt*	Your credit card has been declined.
ID, takk. *ee·deh tahk*	ID, please.
Vi tar ikke kredittkort. *vee tahr ihke kreh·diht·kurt*	We don't accept credit cards.
Kun kontant, takk. *kewn kun·tahnt tahk*	Cash only, please.
Har du mindre sedler? *hahr dew mihn´· druh sehd´·luhr*	Do you have any smaller change?

Services

Can you recommend...?	**Kan du anbefale...?** *kahn dew <u>ahn</u>`·buh·**fah**·luh...*
a barber	**en herrefrisør** *ehn <u>hehr</u>`·ruh·frih·s**urr**
a dry cleaner	**et renseri** *eht rehn·suh·<u>**ree**´</u>
a hairdresser	**en frisørsalong** *ehn frih·s**ur**´r·sah·lohng*
a laundromat [launderette]	**et vaskeri** *eht vahs·kuh·<u>**ree**´</u>
a nail salon	**en neglesalong** *ehn <u>nay</u>`·luh·sah·lohng*
a spa	**et spa** *eht spah*
a travel agency	**et reisebyrå** *eht <u>ray</u>`·suh·bui·r**aw**
Can you... this?	**Kan du...denne/dette?** *kahn dew... <u>dehn</u>`·nuh/<u>deht</u>`·tuh*
alter	**sy om** *sui ohm*
clean	**rense** *<u>rehn</u>`·suh*
mend	**lappe** *<u>lah</u>`·puh*
press	**presse** *<u>prehs</u>`·suh*
When will it be ready?	**Når er den/det ferdig?** *nohr ar dehn/deh <u>fa</u>`·r·dih*

For Grammar, see page 165.

Hair & Beauty

I'd like...	**Jeg vil gjerne ha...** *yay vihl <u>ya</u>`r·nuh hah...*
an appointment for today/ tomorrow	**en time i dag/i morgen** *ehn <u>tee</u>`·muh ih d**ah**g/ih <u>maw</u>`·ruhn*
I'd like...	**Jeg vil gjerne ha...** *yay vihl <u>ya</u>`r·nuh hah...*
an eyebrow/ bikini wax	**voksing av øyenbrynene/bikinilinjen** *<u>vohk</u>`·sihng ah <u>ury</u>`·uhn·bruin·uh·nuh/bih·<u>kee</u>´·nih·lihn·yuhn*
a facial	**en ansiktsbehandling** *ehn <u>ahn</u>`·sihkts·buh·hahnd·lihng*

Many luxury hotels in Norway offer spa and other health and beauty treatments. **Geilo** (www.geilo.no) is a popular health and wellness retreat where you can also enjoy excellent skiing.

a manicure/ pedicure	**manikyr/fotpleie**	mah·nih·<u>kui</u>´r/<u>foot</u>`·play·uh
a massage	**massasje**	mahs·<u>sah</u>`·shuh
some color	**litt farge**	liht <u>fahr</u>`·guh
some highlights	**noen striper**	<u>noo</u>`·uhn <u>str<u>ee</u></u>`·puhr
my hair styled	**håret stylet**	<u>haw</u>´·ruh <u>stiel</u>`·uht
a hair cut	**en klipp**	ehn klihp
a trim	**en stuss**	ehn stews
Don't cut it too short.	**Klipp det ikke for kort.**	klip deh <u>ihk</u>`·kuh fohr kohrt
Shorter here.	**Kortere her.**	<u>kohr</u>`·tuhr·uh h<u>a</u>r
Do you do…?	**Tilbyr dere…?**	<u>tihl</u>´·b<u>ui</u>r <u>deh</u>`·ruh…
acupuncture	**akupunktur**	ah·kew·pewngk·<u>tew</u>´r
aromatherapy	**aromaterapi**	ah·<u>roo</u>´·mah·teh·rah·p<u>ee</u>
oxygen treatment	**surstoffbehandling**	<u>sew</u>´r·stohf·buh·hahnd·lihng
Is there a sauna?	**Fins det sauna?**	fihns deh <u>sev</u>´·nah

Antiques

How old is this?	**Hvor gammel er den?**	*voor <u>gahm</u>•muhl ar dehn*
Do you have anything of the…era?	**Har du noe fra…tiden?**	*hahr dew <u>noo</u>`•uh fra… <u>tee</u>`•duhn*
Do I have to fill out any forms?	**Må jeg fylle ut noen skjemaer?**	*maw yay fyll•eh ewt nu•ehn sheh•mah•ehr*
Will I have problems with customs?	**Tror du jeg kan få problemer i tollen?**	*troor dew yay kahn faw pru•<u>bleh</u>`•muhr ih <u>tohl</u>`•luhn*
Is there a certificate of authenticity?	**Har du et ekthetssertifikat?**	*hahr dew et <u>ehkt</u>`•hehts•ser•tih•fih•kat*
Can you ship/wrap it?	**Kan du sende den/pakke den inn?**	*kahn dew <u>seh</u>`•nuh dehn/<u>pahk</u>`•kuh dehn ihn*

Clothing

I'd like…	**Jeg vil gjerne…**	*yay vihl <u>yar</u>`•nuh…*
Can I try this on?	**Kan jeg prøve den?**	*kahn yay <u>prur</u>`•vuh dehn*
It doesn't fit.	**Den passer ikke.**	*dehn <u>pahs</u>`•suhr <u>ihk</u>`•kuh*
It's too…	**Den er for…**	*dehn ar fohr…*
big/ small	**stor/liten**	*<u>lee</u>`•tuhn/ stoor*
short/long	**kort/lang**	*kohrt/lahng*
tight/loose	**trang/stor**	*trahng/stur*
Do you have this in size…?	**Har du denne i størrelse…?**	*hahr dew <u>dehn</u>`•nuh ih <u>sturr</u>`•rehl•suh…*
Do you have this… in a bigger/smaller size?	**Har du denne… i større/mindre størrelse?**	*hahr dew <u>dehn</u>`•nuh… ih <u>sturr</u>`•ruh/<u>mihn</u>`•druh <u>sturr</u>•rehl•suh*

Colors

I'd like something in…	**Jeg vil gjerne ha noe i…**	*yay vihl <u>yar</u>`•nuh hah <u>noo</u>`•uh ih…*
beige	**beige**	*behsh*
black	**svart**	*svahrt*

blue	**blått** *bloht*
brown	**brunt** *brewnt*
gray	**grått** *groht*
green	**grønt** *grurnt*
orange	**oransje** *u·rahng´·shuh*
pink	**rosa** *roo´·sah*
purple	**fiolett** *fih·u·leht´*
red	**rødt** *rurt*
white	**hvitt** *viht*
yellow	**gult** *gewlt*

YOU MAY HEAR...

Den kledde deg veldig godt. *dehn klehd·eh day vehl·dihg gawt*   That looks great on you.

Hvordan passer den? *voor·dahn pahs·ehr dehn*   How does it fit?

Vi har ikke din størrelse. *vee hahr ihk·eh dihn sturr·als·eh*   We don't have your size.

Clothes & Accessories

backpack	**en ryggsekk** *ehn ruig`•sehk*
belt	**et belte** *eht behl`•tuh*
bikini	**en bikini** *ehn bih•kee´•nih*
blouse	**en bluse** *ehn blew`•suh*
bra	**en behå** *ehn beh`•haw*
briefs [underpants]	**en underbukse** *ehn ewn`•uhr•buk•suh*
coat	**en frakk m /kåpe f** *ehn frahk/kaw`•puh*
dress	**en kjole** *ehn khoo`•luh*
hat	**en hatt** *ehn haht*
jacket	**en jakke** *ehn yahk`•kuh*
jeans	**en olabukse** *ehn oo`•lah•buk•suh*
pajamas	**en pyjamas** *ehn pui•shah´•mahs*
pants [trousers]	**en langbukse** *ehn lahng`•buk•suh*
panties (for women's underwear)	**undertøy** *ewnd•ar•tury*
panty hose [tights]	**en strømpebukse** *ehn strurm`•puh•buk•suh*
purse [handbag]	**en håndveske** *ehn hohn`•vehs•kuh*
raincoat	**en regnfrakk** *ehn rayn`•frahk*
scarf	**et skjerf** *eht shehrf*
shirt	**en skjorte** *ehn shoor`•tuh*

shorts	**et par shorts** *eht pahr shawrts*
skirt	**et skjørt** *eht shurrt*
socks	**et par sokker** *eht pahr sohk`·kuhr*
stockings	**et par strømper** *eht pahr strurm`·puhr*
suit	**en dress** *m* **/drakt** *f* *ehn drehss/drahkt*
sunglasses	**solbriller** *soo`l·brihl·luhr*
sweater	**en genser** *ehn gehn´·suhr*
sweat suit	**en treningsdrakt** *ehn treh`·nihngs·drahkt*
swimming trunks	**en badebukse** *ehn bah`·duh-buk·suh*
swimsuit	**en badedrakt** *ehn bah`·duh·drahkt*
T-shirt	**en T-skjorte** *ehn teh´·shu·rtuh*
tie	**et slips** *eht shlips*
undershirt	**en trøye** *ehn trury·uh*

Fabric

I'd like...	**Jeg vil gjerne ha...** *yay vihl yar`·nuh hah...*
cotton	**bomull** *bum`·mewl*
denim	**denim** *deh´·nihm*
lace	**knipling** *knihp`·lihng*
leather	**lær** *lar*
linen	**lin** *leen*
silk	**silke** *sihl`·kuh*
wool	**ull** *ewl*
Is it machine washable?	**Kan den vaskes i maskin?** *kahn dehn vahs`·kuhs ih mah·shee´n*

Shoes

I'd like...	**Jeg vil gjerne ha...** *yay vihl yar`·nuh hah...*
boots	**støvler** *sturv`·luhr*
flat shoes	**lavhælte sko** *lahv`·hehl·tuh skoo*
high heels	**sko med høye hæler** *skoo meh hury`·uh heh`luhrl*
loafers	**mokkasiner** *muk·kah·see´·nuhr*

sandals	**sandaler** *sahn·<u>dah</u>´·luhr*
shoes	**sko** *skoo*
slippers	**tøfler** *turf´·luhr*
sneakers	**turnsko** *tewrn´·skoo*
In size…	**I størrelse…** *ih <u>sturr</u>`·rehl·suh…*

For Numbers, see page 170.

Sizes

small (S)	**liten** <u>lee</u>`·tuhn*
medium (M)	**mellomstor** <u>mehl</u>`·ohm·stoor*
large (L)	**stor** *stoor*
extra large (XL)	**ekstra stor** *<u>ehks</u>´·trah stoor*
petite	**liten (klesstørrelse)** *leet·ehn kleh·sturr·ehls·eh*
plus size	**ekstra stor** *ehk·strah stur*

Newsagent & Tobacconist

Do you sell English-language books/newspapers?	**Har dere bøker/aviser på engelsk?** *hahr deh`·ruh <u>bur</u>´·kuhr/ah·<u>vee</u>´·suhr poh <u>ehng</u>´·ehlsk*
I'd like…	**Jeg vil gjerne ha…** *yay vihl <u>yar</u>`·nuh hah…*
candy [sweets]	**noen godter** *<u>noo</u>`·uhn <u>goht</u>`·tuhr*
chewing gum	**en pakke tyggegummi** *ehn <u>pahk</u>`·kuh <u>tuig</u>`·guh·gew·mi*
a chocolate bar	**en sjokoladeplate** *ehn shu·ku·<u>lah</u>`·duh·p<u>lah</u>·tuh*
cigars	**noen sigarer** *<u>noo</u>`·uhn sih·<u>gah</u>´·ruhr*
a pack/carton of cigarettes	**en pakke/kartong sigaretter** *ehn <u>pahk</u>`·kuh/kahr·<u>tohng</u>´ sih·gah·<u>reht</u>´·tuhr*
a lighter	**en lighter** *ehn <u>lie</u>´·tuhr*
a magazine	**et blad** *eht blah*
matches	**fyrstikker** *<u>fuir</u>`·stihk·kuhr*

a newspaper	**en avis** *ehn ah•vee´s*
a road/town map of...	**et veikart/bykart over...** *eht vay`•kahrt/bui´•kahrt aw•vuhr...*
stamps	**noen frimerker** *noo`•uhn free´•mehr•kuhr*

Photography

I'd like...camera.	**Jeg vil gjerne ha...** *yay vihl yar`•nuh hah...*
an automatic	**et helautomatisk kamera** *eht hehl´•ev•tu•mah•tihsk kah´•meh•rah*
a digital	**et digitalkamera** *eht dih•gih•tah´l•kah•meh•rah*
a disposable	**et engangskamera** *eht ehn´•gangs•kah•meh•rah*
I'd like...	**Jeg vil gjerne ha...** *yay vihl yar`•nuh•hah...*
a battery	**et batteri** *eht baht•tuh•ree´*
digital prints	**papirkopi av digitale bilder** *pah•pee´r•ku•pee ah dih•gih•tah´•luh bihl`•duhr*
a memory card	**en minnebrikke** *ehn mihn´•nuh•brihk•kuh*
Can I print digital photos here?	**Lager dere papirkopier av digitale bilder?** *lah`•guhr deh´•ruh pah•pee´r•ku•pih•uhr ah dih•gih•tah´•luh bihl`•duhr*

Souvenirs

(rose-painted) bowl	**(rosemalt) bolle**	_(roo_`·suh·m_ahlt_) _bohl_´·luh
candlestick	**lysestake**	_lui_`·suh·st_ah_·kuh
cardigan (with Norwegian design)	**lusekofte**	_lew_`·suh·kohf·tuh
doll in native costume	**dukke med bunad**	_dewk_`·kuh meh b_ew_`·nahd
drinking horn	**drikkehorn**	_drihk_`·kuh·h_oo_rn
hunting knife	**jaktkniv**	_yahkt_´·kn_ee_v
plate	**asjett**	ah·_sheht_´
reindeer skin	**reinsdyrskinn**	_reins_´·d_ui_r·shihn
sealskin slippers	**selskinnstøfler**	_sehl_`·shihns·turf·luhr
troll	**troll**	_trohl_
Viking ship	**vikingskip**	_vee_`·kihng·sheep
wooden figurine	**trefigur**	_treh_`·fih·gewr
woven runner	**rye**	_rui_`·uh
Something typically Norwegian, please.	**Jeg vil gjerne ha noe typisk norsk.**	yei vihl yar`·nuh hah n_oo_`·uh t_ui_´·pihsk norsk
Can I see this/that?	**Kan jeg få se på denne/den der?**	kahn yei foh s_eh_ poh _dehn_`·nuh/dehn d_a_r

Typical souvenirs from Norway include knit items like sweaters and cardigans, gloves and mittens. Other handcrafted pieces like silver, glassware, pottery and hand-painted wooden objects, such as bowls with rose designs, Norwegian trolls, fjord horses and viking ships abound. Art lovers will find that there are also many art galleries across the country. It is a good idea to get local recommendations on where to buy. Goat and reindeer skins as well as furs are also popular.

It's the one in the window/display case.	**Det er den i vinduet/monteren.** *deh ar dehn ih* <u>*vihn*</u>`*·dew·uh/*<u>*mohn*</u>´*·tuhr·uhn*
I'd like...	**Jeg vil gjerne ha...** *yei vihl* <u>*yar*</u>`*·nuh hah...*
a battery	**et batteri** *eht baht·tuh·*<u>*ree*</u>´
a bracelet	**et armbånd** *eht* <u>*ahrm*</u>`*·bohn*
a brooch	**en brosje** *ehn* <u>*broh*</u>`*·shuh*
earrings	**et par øreringer** *eht pahr* <u>*ur*</u>´*·ruh·rihng·uhr*
a necklace	**et halskjede** *eht* <u>*hahl*</u>`*s·kheh·duh*
a ring	**en ring** *ehn rihng*
a watch	**en klokke** *ehn* <u>*klohk*</u>`*·kuh*
copper	**kobber** <u>*kohb*</u>`*·buhr*
crystal	**krystall** *krui·*<u>*stahl*</u>´
diamond	**diamant** *dih·ah·*<u>*mahnt*</u>´
white/yellow gold	**hvitt/gult gull** *viht/gewlt gewl*
pearl	**perle** <u>*par*</u>`*·luh*
pewter	**tinn** *tihn*
platinum	**platina** <u>*plah*</u>´*·tih·nah*
sterling silver	**sterlingsølv** <u>*star*</u>´*·lihng·surl*
Is this real?	**Er den ekte?** *ar dehn* <u>*ehk*</u>`*·tuh*
Can you engrave it?	**Kan du få den gravert?** *kahn dew foh dehn grah·*<u>*vehrt*</u>´

Sport & Leisure

ESSENTIAL

When's the game?	**Når går kampen?**	*nohr gawr <u>kahm</u>´•puhn*
Where's...?	**Hvor er...?**	*voor ar...*
the beach	**stranden**	*<u>strahn</u>´•nuhn*
the park	**parken**	*<u>pahr</u>´•kuhn*
the swimming pool	**svømmebassenget**	*<u>svurm</u>`•muh•bahs•sehng•uh*
Is it safe to swim/ dive here?	**Er det trygt å svømme/dykke her?**	*<u>ar</u> deh truikt aw <u>svurm</u>`•muh/<u>duik</u>`•kuh har*
Can I rent [hire] golf clubs?	**Kan jeg leie golfkøller?**	*kahn yay <u>lay</u>`•uh <u>gohlf</u>´•kurl•luhr*
How much per hour?	**Hvor mye koster det per time?**	*voor <u>mui</u>`•uh <u>kohs</u>`•tuhr deh pehr <u>tee</u>´•muh*
How far is it to...?	**Hvor langt er det til...?**	*voor <u>lahngt</u>´ <u>ar</u> deh tihl...*
Can you show me on the map?	**Kan du vise meg det på kartet?**	*kahn dew <u>vee</u>`•suh may deh poh <u>kahr</u>´•tuh*

Watching Sport

When's...?	**Når går...?**	*nohr gawr...*
the basketball game	**basketballkampen**	*<u>bah</u>´s•kuht•bahl•kahm•puhn*
the cycling race	**sykkelløpet**	*<u>suik</u>´•kuhl•<u>lur</u>•puh*
the golf tournament	**golfturneringen**	*<u>gohlf</u>´•tewr•neh•rihng•uhn*
the soccer [football] game	**fotballkampen**	*<u>foot</u>`•bahl•kahm•puhn*
the tennis match	**tenniskampen**	*<u>tehn</u>´•nihs•kahm•puhn*

the volleyball game	**volleyballkampen** _vohl´·lih·bahl·kahm·puhn_
Which teams are playing?	**Hvilke lag spiller?** _vihl´·kuh lahg spihl·luhr_
Where's the stadium?	**Hvor er stadion?** _voor ar stah´d·yohn_
Where can I place a bet?	**Hvor kan jeg spille på hester?** _voor kahn yay spihl`·luh poh hehs`·tuhr_

Norwegians are very active people and particularly enjoy outdoor sports. Water sports, such as boating, canoeing and fishing are popular, though skiing and hiking are the primary participant sports. In fact, Norwegians boast 4,000 years of skiing, since skis were originally developed as a means of transportation through the snow. Today, there are many ski resorts across Norway and tourist offices can recommend the nearest one for downhill skiing as well as local ski facilities for cross-country skiing. Hiking can be done almost anywhere, but if you're up for an exhilarating experience, try **brevandringer** (guided glacier walks).

Playing Sport

Where's...?	**Hvor er...?** *voor ar...*
the golf course	**golfbanen** _gohlf´_•*bah•nuh*
the gym	**trimrommet** _trihm´_•*rum•muh*
the park	**parken** _pahr´_•*kuhn*
the tennis court	**tennisbanen** _tehn´_•*nihs•bah•nuhn*
How much per...?	**Hva koster det per...?** *vah* _kohs`_•*tuhr deh pehr...*
day	**dag** *dahg*
hour	**time** _tee`_•*muh*
game	**spill** *spihl*
round	**runde** _rewn`_•*duh*
Can I rent [hire]...?	**Kan man leie...?** *kahn mahn* _lay`_•*uh...*
golf clubs	**golfkøller** _gohlf´_•*kurl•luhr*
equipment	**utstyr** _ew`t_•*stuir*
a racket	**en racket** *ehn* _rehk´_•*kuht*

Skiing is the most popular participant sport in Norway and the
winter season runs from November to April. Summer skiing is
also posisble from June to September in some high altitude resorts
where mornings swooshing down the slopes can be combined with
afternoon sunbathing. Major ski resorts are located in Geilo, Hafjell,
Hemsedal, Lillehammer, Norefjell (the closest to Oslo) and Trysil. Other
snow-oriented activities include dog-sledding, ice-fishing, skating,
sleigh-riding, snowboarding, snowmobiling and tobogganing.

At the Beach/Pool

Where's the beach/ pool?	**Hvor er stranden/svømmebassenget?** _voor ar strahn`·nuhn/svurm`·muh·bah·sehng·uh_
Is there...here?	**Fins det...her?** _fihns deh...har_
a kiddie [paddling] pool	**et barnebasseng** _eht bahr`·nuh·bahs·sehng_
an indoor/ outdoor pool	**et innendørs/utendørs svømmebasseng** _eht ihn`·nuhn·durrs/ ew`·tuhn·durrs svurm`·muh·bahs·sehng_
a lifeguard	**badevakt** _bah`·duh·vahkt_
Is it safe...here?	**Er det trygt...her?** _ar deh truikt...har_
to swim	**å svømme** _oh svurm`·muh_
to dive	**å dykke** _oh duik`·kuh_
for children	**for barn** _fohr bahn_
I want to rent [hire]...	**Jeg vil gjerne leie...** _yay vihl yar`·nuh lay`·uh..._
a deck chair	**en fluktstol** _ehn flewkt`·stool_
diving equipment	**dykkeutstyr** _duik`·kuh·ewt·stuir_
a jet-ski	**en vannscooter** _ehn vahn`·skew·tuhr_

On good summer days the temperatures in Norway can be warm enough to sunbathe and swim. There are possibilities for diving, waterskiing and windsurfing along the coast and on Norway's many lakes. White-water rafting and kayaking are an adrenaline-pumping option on the rivers in Oppland, Hedmark and Sør-Trøndelag.

a motorboat	**en motorboat** ehn <u>moo</u>´•toor•bawt
a rowboat	**en robåt** <u>ehn roo</u>´•bawt
snorkling equipment	**snorkleutstyr** <u>snohr</u>`k•luh•**ewt**•stuir
a surfboard	**et surfebrett** eht <u>sewr</u>`•fuh•breht
a towel	**et håndkle** eht <u>hohng</u>`•kleh
an umbrella	**en parasoll** ehn pah•rah•<u>sohl</u>´
water-skis	**vannski** <u>vahn</u>`•sh**ee**
For…hours.	**For…timer.** fohr… <u>tee</u>`•muhr

For Traveling with Children, see page 147.

Winter Sports

Can I have a lift pass for a day/five days?	**Kan jeg få et heiskort for én dag/fem dager?** kahn yay faw eht <u>hays</u>`•kort fohr **eh**n dahg/fehm <u>dah</u>`•g•uhr
I'd like to rent [hire]…	**Jeg vil gjerne leie…** yay vihl <u>yar</u>`•nuh <u>lay</u>`•uh…
boots	**støvler** <u>sturv</u>`•luhr
a helmet	**en hjelm** ehn yehlm
poles	**staver** <u>stah</u>`•vuhr
skis	**ski** shee
a snowboard	**et snøbrett** eht <u>snur</u>`•breht
snowshoes	**truger** <u>trew</u>`•guhr

These are too big/small.	**Disse er for store/små.** _dihs`•suh_ ar fohr <u>stoo</u>´•ruh/ smaw
Can I take skiing lessons?	**Kan jeg ta skitimer?** kahn yay tah <u>shee</u>´•tee•muhr
I'm a beginner.	**Jeg er nybegynner.** yay ar <u>nui</u>`•buh•yuin•nuhr
Can I have a trail [piste] map?	**Kan jeg få et løypekart?** kahn yay faw eht <u>lury</u>`•puh•kahrt

Out in the Country

Can I have a map of…?	**Kan jeg få et kart over…?** kahn yay faw eht kart <u>aw</u>´•vuhr…
this region	**dette området** <u>deht</u>`•tuh <u>ohm</u>´•raw•duh
the walking routes	**turstier** <u>tewr</u>´•stee•uhr
the bike routes	**sykkelstier** <u>suik</u>´•kuhl•stee•uhr
the trails	**skiløypene** <u>shee</u>´•lury•puh•nuh
Is it an easy/a difficult trip?	**Er det en lett/vanskelig tur?** ar deh ehn leht/ <u>vahn</u>`•skuh•lih tewr
Is it far/steep?	**Er det langt/bratt?** ar deh lahngt/braht

How far is it to…?	**Hvor langt er det til…?**	
	voor lahngt´ ar deh tihl. . .	
Can you show me on the map?	**Kan du vise meg på kartet?** *kahn dew vee`·suh may poh kahr´·tuh*	
I'm lost.	**Jeg har gått meg bort.**	
	yay hahr goht may bu·rt	
Where's…?	**Hvor er…?** *voor ar. . .*	
the bridge	**broen** *broo´·uhn*	
the cave	**hulen** *hew`·luhn*	
the farm	**gården** *gawr´·uhn*	
the ferry landing	**ferjestedet** *fer`·yuh·steh·duh*	
the field	**jordet** *yoo`·ruh*	
the fjord	**fjorden** *fyoo`·ruhn*	
the forest	**skogen** *skoo´·guhn*	
the glacier	**breen** *breh´·uhn*	
the hill	**bakken** *bahk`·kuhn*	
the lake	**innsjøen** *ihn`·shur·uhn*	
the mountain	**fjellet** *fyehl´·luh*	
the nature preserve	**nasjonalparken** *nah·shu·nah´l·par·kuhn*	

the overlook	**utsikten** _ew`t•sihk•tuhn_
the park	**parken** _pahr´•kuhn_
the path	**stien** _stee´•uhn_
the peak	**toppen** _tohp´•puhn_
the picnic area	**turområdet** _tewr´•um•raw•duh_
the pond	**dammen** _dahm´•muhn_
the river	**elva** _ehl´•vah_
the waterfall	**fossen** _foh´•suhn_

Culturally, there is a lot to enjoy in Norway. In summer, many
cultural events, including orchestral concerts and operas, are
celebrated outdoors. Theater is extremely popular, though most
productions are in Norwegian. Classical ballet is performed at the Oslo
Opera House and traditional folk dances can be seen across the country.
If you are interested in the visual arts, the Munch museum, named
after the internationally-famous Edvard Munch, in Oslo is popular. The
extensive National Museum of Art, Architecture and Design is also in Oslo.

Going Out

ESSENTIAL

What is there to do at night?	**Hva kan man gjøre om kvelden?** *vah kahn mahn yur`•ruh ohm kvehl´•uhn*
Do you have a program of events?	**Har du en oversikt over ting som skjer?** *hahr dew ehn aw`•vuhr•sihkt aw´•vuhr tihng sohm shehr*
What's playing at the movies [cinema] tonight?	**Hvilke filmer vises på kino i kveld?** *vihl`•kuh fihl`•muhr vee´•suhs poh khee´•nu ih kvehl*
Where's...?	**Hvor er...?** *voor ar...*
the downtown area	**sentrum** *sehn´•trewm*
the bar	**baren** *bahr´•uhn*
the dance club	**diskoteket** *dihs•ku•teh´•kuh*
What's the admission charge?	**Hva koster det å komme inn?** *vah kohs`•tuhr deh oh kohm`•muh ihn*

Entertainment

Can you recommend...?	**Kan du anbefale...?** *kahn dew ahn´•buh•fah•luh...*
a concert	**en konsert** *ehn kohn•sehrt´*
a movie	**en film** *ehn fihlm*
an opera	**en opera** *ehn oo´•puh•rah*
a play	**et teaterstykke** *eht teh•ah´•tuhr•stuik•kuh*
When does it start/end?	**Når begynner/slutter det?** *norh buh•yuin´•nuhr/ slew`•tuhr deh*
What's the dress code?	**Hvordan bør man være kledt?** *voor´•dahn burr mahn va`•ruh kleht*

I like...	**Jeg liker...** _yay <u>lee</u>´·kuhr..._
classical music	**klassisk musikk** _<u>klahs</u>´·sihsk mew·<u>sihk</u>´_
folk music	**folkemusikk** _<u>fohl</u>`·kuh·mew·sihk_
jazz	**jazz** _yahs_
pop music	**pop** _pohp_
rap	**rap** _rehp_

YOU MAY HEAR...

Vennligst skru av alle mobiltelefoner.
<u>vehn</u>´·lihkst skr**ew ah** <u>ahl</u>`·luh mu·<u>bee</u>´l·tehl·uh·**foo**·nuhr

Turn off your cell [mobile] phones.

Nightlife

What is there to do at night?	**Hva kan man gjøre om kvelden?** _vah kahn mahn <u>yur</u>`·ruh um <u>kvehl</u>´·uhn_
Can you recommend...?	**Kan du anbefale...?** _kahn d**ew** <u>ahn</u>´·buh·**fah**·luh..._

The capital offers endless options for going out in pubs, bars, cafes and nightclubs. Many clubs offer live music and attract DJs and musicians from around the world. Oslo also has a growing jazz scene. All restaurants, bars and nightclubs are smoke-free indoors, though many set up outdoor tables in summer and protection for smokers in the winter. Keep in mind that alcohol is considerably more expensive in Norway than in other countries and many clubs enforce age restrictions.

a cabaret	**en kabaret** *ehn kahb•ahr•eh*
a club with . . . . Music	**en nattklubb med ... Musikk** *ehn naht•klewb meh mews•ihk*
a dance club	**et diskotek** *eht dihs•ku•teh´k*
a gay club	**en homseklubb** *ehn hum`•suh•klewb*
a nightclub	**en nattklubb** *naht`•klewb*
Is there live music?	**Er det levende musikk der?** *ar deh leh`•vuhn•uh mew•sihk´ dar*
How do I get there?	**Hvordan kommer jeg dit?** *voor´•dahn kohm´•muhr yay deet*
What's the admission charge?	**Hva koster det å komme inn?** *vah kohs`•tuhr deh oh kohm`•muh ihn*
Let's go dancing.	**La oss gå ut og danse.** *lah ohs gaw ewt oh dahn`•suh*
Is this area safe at night?	**Er dette området trygt om natten?** *ar deht•eh awm•rawd•eht trygt awm naht•ehn*

Special Requirements

Business Travel

ESSENTIAL

I'm here on business.	**Jeg er her i forretninger.**	*yay ar har ih fohr•<u>reht</u>´•ning•uhr*
Here's my business card.	**Her har du visittkortet mitt.**	*hah hahr dew vih•<u>siht</u>´•kor•tuh miht*
Can I have your card?	**Kan jeg få kortet ditt?**	*kahn yay faw <u>kor</u>´•tuh diht*
I have a meeting with…	**Jeg har et møte med…**	*yay hahr eht <u>mur</u>`•tuh meh…*
Where's…?	**Hvor er…?**	*voor ar…*
the business center	**forretningssenteret**	*fohr•<u>reht</u>´•nihngs•sehn•tuhr•uh*
the convention hall	**konferansesenteret**	*kohn•fehr•<u>ahng</u>´•suh•sehn•tuhr•uh*
the meeting room	**møterommet**	*<u>mur</u>`•tuh•rum•muh*

On Business

I'm here to attend…	**Jeg er her for å delta i…**	*yay ar har fohr aw <u>deh</u>`•l•tah ih…*
a seminar	**et seminar**	*eht seh•mih•<u>nah</u>´r*
a conference	**en konferanse**	*ehn kohn•fehr•<u>ahng</u>´•suh*
a meeting	**et møte**	*eht <u>mur</u>`•te*
My name is…	**Jeg heter…**	*yay <u>heh</u>`•tuhr…*
May I introduce my colleague…	**La meg få presentere min kollega…**	*lah may foh preh•sahng•<u>teh</u>´•ruh mihn kohl•<u>leh</u>´•gah…*
Nice to meet you!	**Hyggelig å treffes!**	*<u>huig</u>`•guh•lih oh <u>trehf</u>´•fuhs*
I have a meeting/an appointment with…	**Jeg har et møte/en avtale med…**	*yay hahr eht <u>mur</u>`•tuh/ehn <u>ah</u>`v•tah•luh meh…*

I'm sorry I'm late.	**Jeg beklager at jeg er sent ute.** *yay buh•klah´•guhr aht yay ar sehnt ew´•tuh*
I need an interpreter.	**Jeg trenger en tolk.** *yay trehng´•uhr ehn tohlk*
You can reach me at the... Hotel.	**Du kan nå meg på Hotell...** *Dew kahn naw may paw hu•tehl´...*
I'm here until...	**Jeg blir her til...** *yay bleer har tihl...*
I need to...	**Jeg trenger å...** *yay trehng´•uhr oh...*
make a call	**ta en telefon** *tah ehn teh•luh•foo´n*
make a photocopy	**ta en kopi** *tah ehn ku•pee´*
send an e-mail	**sende en e-post** *sehn`•nuh ehn eh´•pohst*
send a fax	**sende en faks** *sehn`•nuh ehn fahks*
send a package (overnight)	**sende en pakke (over natten)** *sehn`•nuh ehn pahk`•kuh (aw´•vuhr naht´•tuhn)*

Norwegians tend to get right to business and don't tend to
engage in much small talk or socializing. You'll find them to
be serious and direct in business dealings, and in their manner of
speaking in general.
Though titles and surnames are used frequently in introductions, they
are usually dropped later. Greetings are accompanied by a handshake.

YOU MAY HEAR...

Har du en avtale? *hahr dew ehn ah`v•tah•luh* — Do you have an appointment?

Med hvem? *meh vehm* — With whom?

Han/Hun er på et møte. *hahn/huhn ar poh eht mur`•tuh* — He/She is in a meeting.

Et øyeblikk. *eht ury`•uh•blihk* — One moment.

Her har du en stol. *har hahr dew ehn stool* — Have a seat.

Vil du ha noe å drikke? *vihl dew hah noo`•uh oh drihk`•kuh* — Would you like something to drink?

Takk for at du kom. *tahk fohr aht dew kohm* — Thank you for coming.

ESSENTIAL

Is there any discount for children?	**Er det reduksjon for barn?** *ar deh reh•dewk•shoo´n fohr bahrn*
Can you recommend a babysitter?	**Kan du anbefale en barnevakt?** *kahn dew ahn´•buh•fah•luh ehn bahr´•nuh•vahkt*
Could we have a child's seat/highchair?	**Kan vi få en barnestol/babystol?** *kahn vee faw ehn bahr´•nuh•stool/beh´•bih•stool*
Where can I change the baby?	**Hvor kan jeg bytte på babyen?** *voor kahn yay buit´•tuh poh beh´•bih•uhn*

Out & About

Can you recommend something for the kids?	**Kan du anbefale noe for barna?** *kahn dew ahn´•buh•fah•luh noo´•uh fohr bahr´•nah*
Where's…?	**Hvor er…?** *voor ar…*
the amusement park	**fornøyelsesparken** *fohr•nury´•uhl•suhs•pahr•kuhn*
the arcade	**spillehallen** *spihl•eh•hahl•ehn*
the kiddie [paddling] pool	**plaskebassenget** *plahs´•kuh•bahs•sehng•uh*
the park	**parken** *pahr´•kuhn*
the playground	**lekeplassen** *leh´•kuh•plahs•suhn*
the zoo	**dyrehagen** *dui´•ruh•hah•guhn*
Are kids allowed?	**Er det adgang for barn?** *ar deh ahd´•gahng fohr bahrn*

Is it safe for children?	**Er det trygt for barn?**	*ar deh truikt fohr bahrn*
Is it suitable for... year olds?	**Passer det for...åringer?**	*pahs`·suhr deh fohr. . .`·awr·ihng·uhr*

For Numbers, see page 170.

Baby Essentials

Do you have...?	**Har dere...?**	*hahr deh`·ruh. . .*
a baby bottle	**en tåteflaske**	*ehn taw`·tuh·flahs·kuh*
baby wipes	**papirkluter**	*pah·pee`r·klew·tuhr*
a car seat	**et barnesete**	*eht bahr`·nuh·seh·tuh*
a children's menu/ portion	**en barnemeny/barneporsjon**	*ehn bahr`·nuh·meh·nui/bahr`·nuh·poor·shoon*
a child's seat/ highchair	**en barnestol/babystol**	*ehn bahr`·nuh·stool/beh´·bih·stool*
a crib/cot	**en barneseng/sprinkelseng**	*ehn bahr`·nuh·sehng/sprihng´·kul·sehng*
diapers [nappies]	**bleier**	*blay`·uhr*
formula	**morsmelkerstatning**	*moors´·mehlk·ehr·staht·nihng*
a pacifier [dummy]	**en narresmokk**	*ehn nahr`·ruh·smuk*
a playpen	**en lekegrind**	*ehn leh`·kuh·grihn*
a stroller [pushchair]	**en gåstol**	*ehn gaw´·stool*

Can I breastfeed the baby here?	**Kan jeg amme babyen her?** *kahn yay <u>ahm</u>`•uh <u>beh</u>´•bih•uhn h*a*r*
Where can I change the baby?	**Hvor kan jeg bytte på babyen?** *voor kahn yay <u>buit</u>`•tuh poh <u>beh</u>´•bih•uhn*

For Dining with Children, see page 63.

Babysitting

Can you recommend a reliable babysitter?	**Kan du anbefale en pålitelig barnevakt?** *kahn d*e*w <u>ahn</u>´•buh•f*a*h•luh ehn poh•<u>lee</u>´•tuh•lih <u>bahr</u>`•nuh•vahkt*
What's the charge?	**Hvor mye koster det?** *voor <u>mui</u>`•uh <u>kohs</u>`•tuhr deh*
We'll be back by…	**Vi er tilbake klokken…** *vee ar tihl•<u>bah</u>`•kuh <u>klohk</u>`•kuhn…*
I'll be back by…	**Jeg er tilbake til…** *yay ar tihl•bahk•<u>eh</u> tih*
I can be reached at…	**Jeg kan nås på…** *yay kahn n*a*ws poh…*
If you need to contact me, call…	**Om du må kontakte meg, ring…** *Awm d*e*w m*a*w kun•takht•<u>eh</u> may <u>rihng</u>*

Health & Emergency

Can you recommend a pediatrician?	**Kan du anbefale en barnelege?** *kahn d*e*w ahn*´*•buh•f*a*h•luh ehn <u>bahr</u>`•nuh•<u>leh</u>•guh*
My child is allergic to…	**Barnet mitt er allergisk mot…** *<u>bahr</u>´•nuh miht ar ah•<u>lehr</u>´•gihsk m*oo*t…*
My child is missing.	**Barnet mitt er kommet bort.** *<u>bahr</u>`•nuh miht ar <u>kohm</u>`•muht boort*
Have you seen a boy/girl?	**Har du sett en gutt/jente?** *<u>hahr</u> dew seht ehn gewt/ <u>yehn</u>`•tuh*

For Police, see page 154.

For Pharmacy, see page 161.

Disabled Travelers

ESSENTIAL

Is there…?	**Er det…?** *ar deh…*
access for the disabled	**adkomst for bevegelseshemmede** <u>*ahd*</u>`*·kohmst fohr buh·*<u>*veh*</u>´*·guhl·suhs·hem·muhd·uh*
a wheelchair ramp	**en rullestolsrampe** *ehn* <u>*rewl*</u>´*·luh·stools·rahm·puh*
a handicapped-[disabled-] accessible toilet	**et handikaptoalett** *eht* <u>*hehn*</u>´*·dih·kehp·tu·ah·leht*
I need…	**Jeg trenger…** *yay* <u>*trehng*</u>´*·uhr…*
assistance	**hjelp** *yehlp*
an elevator [lift]	**en heis** *ehn hays*
a ground-floor room	**et rom i første etasje** *eht rum ih* <u>*furr*</u>`*·stuh eh·*<u>*tah*</u>´*·shuh*

Asking for Assistance

I'm disabled.	**Jeg er bevegelseshemmet.** *yay ar buh·*<u>*veh*</u>´*·guhl·suhs·hem·muht*
I'm visually/hearing impaired.	**Jeg er synshemmet/hørselshemmet.** *yay ar* <u>*sui*</u>´*ns·hehm·muht/*<u>*hurr*</u>´*·sehls·hehm·muht*
I'm unable to walk far.	**Jeg kan ikke gå langt.** *yay kahn* <u>*ihk*</u>`*·kuh gaw lahngt*
I'm unable to use the stairs.	**Jeg kan ikke bruke trappen.** *yay kahn* <u>*ihk*</u>`*·kuh* <u>*brew*</u>`*·kuh* <u>*trahp*</u>´*·puhn*

Can I bring my wheelchair? **Kan jeg komme i rullestol?** *kahn yay <u>kohm`</u>•muh ih <u>rewl`</u>•luh•stool*

Are guide dogs permitted? **Er det adgang for førerhunder?** *ar deh <u>ahd`</u>•gahng fohr <u><b>fur`</u>•ruhr•hewn•nuhr*

Can you help me? **Kan du hjelpe meg?** *kahn dew <u>yehl`</u>•puh may*

Can you open/hold the door? **Kan du åpne/holde døra?** *kahn dew <u>awp`</u>•nuh/ <u>hohl`</u>•luh <u>dur´</u>•rah*

In an Emergency

Emergencies

ESSENTIAL

Help!	**Hjelp!** *yehlp*
Go away!	**Gå vekk!** *gaw vehk*
Stop, thief!	**Stopp tyven!** *stohp tui´•vuhn*
Get a doctor!	**Hent en lege!** *hehnt ehn leh`•guh*
Fire!	**Brann!** *brahn*
I'm lost.	**Jeg har gått meg bort.**
	yay hahr goht may boort
Can you help me?	**Kan du hjelpe meg?**
	kahn dew yehl`•puh may

In an emergency, dial: **112** for the police.
110 for the fire brigade
113 for medical emergencies.

Police

ESSENTIAL

Call the police!	**Ring politiet!** *ring pu·lih·tee´·uh*
Where's the police station?	**Hvor er politistasjonen?** *voor ar pu·lih·tee´·stah·shoo·nuhn*
There's been an accident/attack.	**Det har skjedd en ulykke/et overfall.** *deh har shehd ehn ew´·luik·kuh/eht aw`·vuhr·fahl*
My child is missing.	**Barnet mitt er kommet bort.** *bahr`·nuh miht ar kohm`·muht boort*
I need...	**Jeg trenger...** *yay trehng´·uhr...*
an interpreter	**en tolk** *ehn tohlk*
to contact my lawyer	**å kontakte advokaten min** *oh kun·tahk´·tuh ahd·vu·kah´·tuhn mihn*
to make a phone call	**å ta en telefon** *oh tah ehn teh·luh·foon´*
I'm innocent.	**Jeg er uskyldig.** *yay ar ew·shuil´·dih*

Crime & Lost Property

I want to report...	**Jeg vil anmelde...** *yay vihl ahn´·meh·luh...*
a mugging	**et overfall** *eht aw`·vuhr·fahl*
a rape	**en voldtekt** *ehn vohl`·tehkt*
a theft	**et tyveri** *eht tui·vuhr·ee´*
I've been robbed/mugged.	**Jeg har blitt ranet/overfalt.** *yay hahr bliht rah`·nuht/aw`·vuhr·fahlt*
I've lost...	**Jeg har mistet...** *yay hahr mihs`·tuht...*
...has been stolen.	**...er blitt stjålet.** *...ar bliht styaw`·luht*

My backpack	**Ryggsekken min**	_ruig_`·sehk·kuhn mihn
My bicycle	**Sykkelen min**	_suik_´·kuhl·uhn mihn
My camera	**Fotoapparatet mitt**	_foo_´·tu·ahp·pah·raht·uh miht
My (rental) car	**(Leie-)bilen min**	_(lay_`·uh)·b**eel**·uhn mihn
My computer	**PCen min**	_peh_`·s**eh**·uhn mihn
My credit cards	**Kredittkortet mitt**	kreh·_diht_´·kor·tuh miht
My jewelry	**Smykkene mine**	_smuik_`·kuh·nuh _mih_`·nuh
My money	**Pengene mine**	_pehng_`·uh·nuh _mih_`·nuh
My passport	**Passet mitt**	_pahs_´·suh miht
My purse [handbag]	**Håndvesken min**	_hohn_`·vehs·kuhn mihn
My traveler's checks [cheques]	**Reisesjekkene mine**	_ray_`·suh·shehk·kuh·nuh _mih_`·nuh
My wallet	**Lommeboken min**	_lum_`·muh·b**oo**·kuhn mihn
I need a police report for my insurance claim.	**Jeg trenger en politirapport til forsikringskravet mitt.**	yay _trehng_´·uhr ehn pu·lih·_tee_´·rahp·pohrt tihl fohr·_sihk_´·rihngs·kr**ah**·vuh miht
Where is the British/American/Irish embassy?	**Hvor er den britiske/amerikanske/irske ambassaden?**	voor ar dehn breet·ihsk·eh/ ahm·ehr·ee·kahn·skeh/eersk·eh ahm·bah·sahd·ehn
I need an interpreter.	**Jeg trenger en tolk.**	yay trehng·_ehr_ ehn _tawlk_

Health

ESSENTIAL

I'm sick [ill].	**Jeg er syk.** *yay ar suik*
I need an English-speaking doctor.	**Jeg trenger en lege som snakker engelsk.** *yay trehng´·uhr ehn <u>leh</u>`·guh sohm <u>snahk</u>`·kuhr ehng´·ehlsk*
It hurts here.	**Det gjør vondt her.** *deh yurr vunt har*
I have a stomachache.	**Jeg har magesmerter.** *yay hahr <u>mah</u>`·guh·smer·tuhr*

Finding a Doctor

Can you recommend a doctor/dentist?	**Kan du anbefale en lege/tannlege?** *kahn dew <u>ahn</u>`·buh·<b>fah</b>·luh ehn <u>leh</u>`·guh/<u>tahn</u>`·leh·guh*
Can the doctor come to see me here?	**Kan legen komme hit og undersøke meg?** *kahn <u>leh</u>`·guhn <u>kohm</u>`·muh heet oh <u>ewn</u>`·nuhr·sur·kuh may*
I need an English-speaking doctor.	**Jeg trenger en lege som snakker engelsk.** *yay trehng´·uhr ehn <u>leh</u>`·guh sohm <u>snahk</u>`·kuhr ehng´·ehlsk*
What are the office hours?	**Når er det kontortid?** *nawr ar deh kun·<u>toor</u>´·teed*
Can I make an appointment...?	**Kan jeg få time...?** *kahn yay faw <u>tee</u>`·muh...*
for today	**i dag** *ih dahg*
for tomorrow	**i morgen** *ih <u>maw</u>`·ruhn*
as soon as possible	**så snart som mulig** *soh snahrt sohm <u>mew</u>`·lih*
It's urgent.	**Det haster.** *deh <u>hahs</u>`·tuhr*

YOU MAY HEAR...

Hva er i veien? *vah ar ih vay´•uhn*
What's wrong?

Er du allergisk mot noe? *ar dew ah•ler´•gihsk moot noo`•uh*
Are you allergic to anything?

Gap opp. *gahp ohp*
Open your mouth.

Pust dypt. *pewst duipt*
Breathe deeply.

Du bør få foretatt en allmenn undersøkelse. *dew burr foh faw`•ruh•taht ehn ahl`•mehn ewn`•nuhr•sur•kuh•uhl•suh*
I want you to go to the hospital.

Symptoms

I'm bleeding.	**Jeg blør.** *yay blurr*	
I'm constipated.	**Jeg har forstoppelse.** *yay hahr fohr•stohp´•puhl•suh*	
I'm dizzy.	**Jeg er svimmel.** *yay ar svihm´•muhl*	
It hurts here.	**Det gjør vondt her.** *deh yurr vunt har*	
I have...	**Jeg har...** *yay hahr...*	
an allergic reaction	**fått en allergisk reaksjon** *foht ehn ah•ler´•gihsk reh•ahk•shoo´n*	
chest pain	**vondt i brystet** *vunt ih bruis´•tuh*	
cramps	**kramper** *krahm•pehr*	
diarrhea	**diaré** *dee•ahr•ehn*	
an earache	**øreverk** *ur`•ruh•vehrk*	
a fever	**feber** *feh´•buhr*	
pain	**smerter** *smer`•tuhr*	
a rash	**utslett** *ew`t•shleht*	
sprained...	**forstuet...** *fohr•stew´•uht...*	
some swelling	**hevelse** *heh`•vuhl•suh*	
a stomachache	**magesmerter** *mah`•guh•smer•tuhr*	
sunstroke	**fått solstikk** *foht soo`l•stihk*	

| I've been sick [ill] for...days. | **Jeg har vært syk i...dager.** *yay hahr vert suik ih... dahg`•uhr* |
| I'm ...months pregnant. | **Jeg er ...måneder gravid** *yay ar mawn•ehd•ehr grah•veed* |

Conditions

I have...	**Jeg har...** *yay hahr...*
asthma	**astma** *ahst´•mah*
arthritis	**leddgikt** _lehd`_•yihkt
high/low blood pressure	**høyt/lavt blodtrykk** *huryt/lahvt bloo`•truik*
a heart condition	**en hjertesykdom** *ehn yer`•tuh•suik•dohm*
I have epilepsy.	**Jeg har epilepsi.** *yay hahr eh•phi•lehp•see*
I'm allergic to antibiotics/penicillin.	**Jeg er allergisk mot antibiotika/penicillin.** *yay ar ah•ler´•gihsk moot ahn•tih•bih•oo´•tih•kah/ peh•nih•sih•leen´*
I'm on...	**Jeg går på...** *yay gawr poh...*

Treatment

Do I need a prescription/ medicine?	**Trenger jeg resept/medisin?** *trehng•ehr yay rehs•ehpt/meh•dee•seen*
Can you prescribe a generic drug [unbranded medication]?	**Kan du skrive resept på en generika?** *kahn dew skrih•vuh reh•sehpt paw ehn gehn•ehri•kah*
Where can I get it?	**Hvor får jeg tak i det?** *voor fawr yay tahk ee deh*

Hospital

| Please notify my family. | **Vær snill å underrette familien min.** *var snihl oh ewn`•nuhr•reht•uh fah•mee´•lyuhn mihn* |

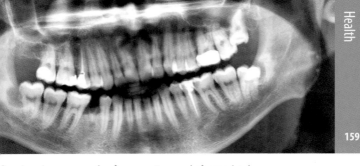

I am in pain.	**Jeg har smerter.** *yay hahr smer`•tuhr*
I need a doctor/nurse.	**Jeg trenger en lege/sykepleier.** *yay trehng´•uhr ehn leh`•guh/sui`•kuh•play•uhr*
What are the visiting hours?	**Når er det besøkstid?** *nohr ar deh buh•sur´ks•teed*
I'm visiting…	**Jeg skal besøke…** *yay skahl buh•sur´k•uh…*

Dentist

I've broken a tooth.	**Jeg har brukket en tann** *yay hahr bruk`•kuht ehn than*
I have lost a filling.	**mistet en plombe.** *yay hahr mihs`•tuht ehn plum`•buh*
I have a toothache.	**Jeg har tannpine.** *yay hahr tahn`•pee•nuh*
Can you fix my dentures?	**Kan du reparere gebisset?** *kahn dew reh•pah•reh´•ruh guh•bihs´•suh*

Gynecologist

I have menstrual cramps/a vaginal infection.	**Jeg har menstruasjonssmerter/underlivsbetennelse.** *yay hahr mehn•strew•ah•shoo´ns•smer•tuhr/ewn`•nuhr•leevs•buh•tehn•nuhl•suh*
I missed my period.	**Jeg har ikke hatt menstruasjon.** *yay hahr ihk`•kuh haht mehn•strew•ah•shoo´n*

I'm on the Pill.	**Jeg tar p-piller.** *yay tahr <u>peh</u>´•pil•luhr*
I'm (not) pregnant.	**Jeg er (ikke) gravid.** *yay ar (<u>ihk</u>`•kuh) grah•<u>vee</u>´d*
I haven't had a period for…months.	**Jeg har ikke hatt menstruasjon på…måneder.** *yay hahr <u>ihk</u>`•kuh haht mehn•strew•ah•<u>shoo</u>´n poh… <u>maw</u>`•nuhd•uhr*

For Numbers, see page 170.

Optician

I've lost…	**Jeg har mistet…** *yay hahr <u>mihs</u>`•tuht…*
a contact lens	**en kontaktlinse** *ehn kun•<u>tahkt</u>´•lihn•suh*
my glasses	**brillene mine** *<u>brihl</u>`•luh•nuh <u>mih</u>`•nuh*
a lens	**et brilleglass** *eht <u>brihl</u>`•luh•glahs*

Payment & Insurance

How much?	**Hvor mye koster det?** *voor <u>mui</u>`•uh <u>kohs</u>`•tuhr deh*
Can I pay by credit card?	**Kan jeg betale med kredittkort?** *kahn yay buh•<u>tah</u>´•luh meh kreh•<u>diht</u>´•kort*
I have insurance.	**Jeg har forsikring.** *yay hahr fohr•<u>sihk</u>´•rihng*
Can I have a receipt for my health insurance?	**Kan jeg få en kvittering for sykeforsikringen?** *kahn yay faw ehn kviht•<u>teh</u>´•rihng fohr <u>sui</u>`k•uh•fohr•sihk•rihng•uhn*

Pharmacy

ESSENTIAL

Where's the nearest pharmacy [chemist's]?	**Hvor er nærmeste apotek?** *voor ar ner`•mehs•tuh ah•pu•teh´k*
What time does the pharmacy [chemist's] open/close?	**Når åpner/stenger apoteket?** *nohr aw`p•nuhr/ stehng`•uhr ah•pu•teh´k•uh*
What would you recommend for...?	**Hva anbefaler du mot...?** *vah ahn´•buh•fah•luhr dew moot...*
How much should I take?	**Hvor mye skal jeg ta?** *voor mui•uh skahl yay tah*
Can you fill [make up] this prescription for me?	**Kan du gjøre i stand denne resepten for meg?** *kahn dew yur`•ruh ih stahn dehn`•nuh reh•sehp´•tuhn fohr may*
I'm allergic to...	**Jeg er allergisk mot...** *yay ar ah•ler´•gihsk moot...*

In Norway, the **apotek** (pharmacy) fills medical prescriptions, while the **parfymeri** (drug store) sells non-prescription items, such as toiletries and cosmetics. Most pharmacies are open during regular business hours: 9:00 a.m. to 6:00 p.m. on weekdays. Certain pharmacies may also be open on weekends and a few are open 24 hours a day.

YOU MAY SEE...

EN GANG/TRE GANGER OM DAGEN	once/three times a day
DRÅPE	drop
TABLETT	tablet
TESKJE	teaspoon
...MÅLTIDER	...meals
ETTER	after
FØR	before
mMED	with
PÅ TOM MAGE	on an empty stomach
Å SVELGE HEL	swallow whole
KAN FORÅRSAKE TRETTHET	may cause drowsiness
IKKE INNTA ORALT	do not ingest
KUN TIL UTVORTES BRUK	for external use only

What to Take

How much should I take?	**Hvor mye skal jeg ta?** *voor mui`•uh skahl yay tah*
How often?	**Hvor ofte?** *voor ohf`•tuh*
I'm taking...	**Jeg tar...** *yay tahr...*
Are there side effects?	**Er det noen bivirkninger?** *ar deh noo`•uhn bee´•vihrk•nihng•uhr*
Is it safe for children?	**Er det trygt for barn?** *ar deht•eh trygt fawr bahn*

Health Problems

I'd like something for...	**Jeg vil gjerne ha noe mot...** *yay vihl yar`•nuh hah noo`•uh moot...*
a cold	**forkjølelse** *fohr•khur´•luhl•suh*
a cough	**hoste** *hus`•tuh*

diarrhea	**diarré**	dih·ah·<u>reh</u>´
insect bites	**insektstikk**	<u>ihn</u>`·sehkt·stihk
motion [travel] sickness	**reisesyke**	<u>ray</u>`·suh·<u>sui</u>·kuh
a sore throat	**sår hals**	sawr hahls
sunburn	**solforbrenning**	<u>soo</u>`l·fohr·brehn·nihng
an upset stomach	**urolig mage**	ew·<u>roo</u>´·lih <u>mah</u>`·guh

Basic Supplies

I'd like…	**Jeg vil gjerne ha…**	yay vihl <u>yar</u>`·nuh hah…
acetaminophen [paracetamol]	**paracetamol**	pah·rah·seht·tahm·<u>oo</u>´l
antiseptic cream	**en antiseptisk salve**	ehn ahn·tih·<u>sehp</u>´·tihsk <u>sahl</u>`·vuh
aspirin	**aspirin**	ahs·pih·<u>ree</u>´n
a bandage [plaster]	**plaster**	<u>plahs</u>´·tuhr
a comb	**en kam**	ehn kahm
condoms	**kondomer**	kun·<u>doo</u>´·muhr
contact lens solution	**kontaktlinsevæske**	kun·<u>tahkt</u>´·lihn·suh·vehs·kuh
deodorant	**en deodorant**	ehn deh·u·du·<u>rahnt</u>´
a hairbrush	**en hårbørste**	ehn <u>haw</u>´r·burr·stuh

hair spray	**hårlakk** _hawr`·lahk_	
ibuprofen	**ibuprofen** _ih·bew·pru·**fehn**´_	
insect repellent	**et insektmiddel** _eht **ihn**`·sehkt·mihd·duhl_	
a nail file	**en neglefil** _ehn nayl`·uh·**feel**_	
a razor/disposable	**en barberhøvel/engangshøvel** _ehn_	
razor	_bahr·**behr**´·hurv·vuhl/**ehn**´·gahngs·hurv·vuhl_	
razor blades	**barberblader** _bahr·**behr**´·blah·uhr_	
sanitary napkins	**sanitetsbind** _sah·nih·**teh**´ts·bihn_	
shampoo/	**en sjampo/hårbalsam** _ehn shahm´·pu/_	
conditioner	_h**aw**`r·bahl·sahm_	
soap	**en såpe** _ehn saw`·puh_	
sunscreen	**solkrem** _soo`l·krehm_	
tampons	**tamponger** _tahm·pohng´·uhr_	
tissues	**papirlommetørklær** _pah·**pee**´r·lum·muh·turrk·luhr_	
toilet paper	**toalettpapir** _tu·ah·**leht**´·pah·peer_	
a toothbrush	**en tannbørste** _ehn tahn`·burr·stuh_	
toothpaste	**en tannpasta** _ehn tahn`·pahst·ah_	

For Baby Essentials, see page 148.

The Basics

Grammar

> Norway has two official written, mutually comprehensible languages, **bokmål** and **nynorsk**. **Bokmål** is the most common and is used throughout this book although a traveler in Norway should expect to come across both.

Verbs

The present tense of regular verbs in Norwegian is formed by adding **-er** to the stem of the verb. The past tense is formed by **-et** or **-te**. The future is formed with **skal** or **vil** + infinitive. This applies to all persons (e.g., I, you, he, she, it, etc.). Following are the present, past and future forms of the verbs **å bytte** (to change) and **å kjøpe** (to buy).

	Present	Past	Future
å bytte (to change)	**bytter**	**byttet**	**skal/vil bytte**
å kjøpe (to buy)	**kjøper**	**kjøpte**	**skal/vil kjøpe**

Irregular Verbs

There are a number of irregular verbs in Norwegian; these must be memorized. Like regular verbs, however, the irregular verb form remains the same, irrespective of person(s). Following are the present, past and future conjugations for a few important, useful irregular verbs.

	Present	Past	Future
å være (to be)	**er**	**var**	**skal/vil være**
å ha (to have)	**har**	**hadde**	**skal/vil ha**
å kunne (to be able to, can)	**kan**	**kunne**	**skal/vil kunne**
å spørre (to ask)	**spør**	**spurte**	**skal/vil spørre**

Imperatives

The imperative is generally the same form as the stem of the verb:

Examples:

Bytt! Change!   **Kjøp!** Buy!   **Gå!** Go!

Nouns

Nouns in Norwegian can be common (masculine/feminine), feminine or neuter. There are no easy rules for determining the gender. It is best to learn each new word with its accompanying article.

The plural of most nouns is formed by an **-(e)r** ending (indefinite plural) or an **-(e)ne** ending (definite plural).

Examples:

common:	**biler**	cars	**bilene**	the cars
neuter:	**epler**	apples	**eplene**	the apples

Many monosyllabic nouns have irregular plurals:

en mann	a man	**menn**	men	**mennene**	the men
en sko	a shoe	**sko**	shoes	**skoene**	the shoes
et hus	a house	**hus**	houses	**husene**	the houses
et barn	a child	**barn**	children	**barna**	the children

Possession is shown by adding **-s** (singular and plural). Note that there is no apostrophe.

Examples:

Johns bror	John's brother
hotellets eier	the owner of the hotel
barnas far	the children's father

Articles

The article (a, an, the) shows the gender of a Norwegian noun, which can be common (masculine/feminine), feminine or neuter.

Note that the majority of feminine nouns also have a common form, but usually appear in their feminine form.

1. Indefinite article (a/an)

common:	**en bil**	a car
feminine:	**en** (or **ei**) **jente**	a girl
neuter:	**et eple**	an apple

2. Definite article (the)

Where in English one says 'the house', Norwegians tag the definite article onto the end of the noun and say 'house-the'. In common nouns 'the' is **-(e)n**, in feminine nouns, **a** and in neuter nouns, **-(e)t**.

Examples:

common:	**bilen**	the car
feminine:	**jenta**	the girl
neuter:	**eplet**	the apple

Personal Pronouns

I	**jeg**
you	**du**
he	**han**
she	**hun**
it	**den/det**
we	**vi**
you (plural)	**dere**
they	**de**

The two forms for 'it' refer to the gender. **Den** refers to masculine and feminine nouns, **det** to neuter nouns.

Norwegian has two forms for 'you': **du** (informal) and **De** (formal). However, today, the use of the formal **De** has practically disappeared from the language.

Negatives

Negation is expressed by using the adverb **ikke** (not). It is usually placed immediately after the verb in a main clause. In compound tenses, **ikke** appears between the auxiliary and the main verb.

Jeg snakker norsk.	I speak Norwegian.
Jeg snakker ikke norsk.	I do not speak Norwegian.

Questions

Questions are generally formed by reversing the order of the subject and the verb:

Examples:

Bussen stanser her.	The bus stops here.
Stanser bussen her?	Does the bus stop here?
Jeg kommer i kveld.	I am coming tonight.
Kommer du i kveld?	Are you coming tonight?

Adjectives

An adjective agrees with the noun it modifies in gender and number. For the indefinite form, the neuter is generally formed by adding **-t**, the plural by adding **-e**.

Examples:

(en) stor hund	(a) big dog	**store hunder**	big dogs
(et) stort hus	(a) big house	**store hus**	big houses

For the definite form of the adjective, add the ending **-e** (common, neuter and plural). This form is used when the adjective is preceded by **den, det, de** (the definite article used with adjectives) or by a demonstrative or a possessive adjective.

Examples:

den store hunden	the big dog
de store hundene	the big dogs
det store huset	the big house
de store husene	the big houses

Comparative & Superlative

The comparative and superlative are normally formed either by adding the ending **-(e)re** and **-(e)st**, respectively, to the adjective, or by putting **mer** (more) and **mest** (most) before the adjective.

Examples:

stor/større/størst	big/bigger/biggest
lett/lettere/lettest	easy/easier/easiest
imponerende/mer imponerende/	impressive/more impressive/
mest imponerende	the most impressive

Demonstrative Adjectives

A demonstrative adjective agrees with the noun it modifies in gender and number. If it doesn't refer to a noun, the neuter form is used, e.g., **Hva er det?** What is that?

	common	neuter	plural
this/these	**denne**	**dette**	**disse**
that/those	**den**	**det**	**de**

Adverbs

Adverbs are often formed by adding -**t** to the corresponding adjective.

rask/raskt	quick/quickly
langsom/langsomt	slow/slowly

NUMBERS

ESSENTIAL

0	**null**	*newl*
1	**en**	*ehn*
2	**to**	*too*
3	**tre**	*treh*
4	**fire**	<u>*fee*</u>*`·ruh*
5	**fem**	*fehm*
6	**seks**	*sehks*
7	**sju**	*shew*
8	**åtte**	<u>*oht*</u>*`·tuh*
9	**ni**	*nee*
10	**ti**	*tee*
11	**elleve**	<u>*ehl*</u>*`·vuh*
12	**tolv**	*tohl*
13	**tretten**	<u>*treh*</u>*`t·tuhn*
14	**fjorten**	<u>*fyu*</u>*`·rtuhn*
15	**femten**	<u>*fehm*</u>*`·tuhn*
16	**seksten**	<u>*says*</u>*`·tuhn*
17	**sytten**	<u>*surt*</u>*`·tuhn*
18	**atten**	<u>*aht*</u>*`·tuhn*
19	**nitten**	<u>*niht*</u>*`·tuhn*
20	**tjue**	<u>*khew*</u>*`·uh*
21	**tjueen**	*khew·uh·*<u>**eh**</u>*´n*
22	**tjueto**	*khew·uh·*<u>*too*</u>*´*
30	**tretti**	<u>*treht*</u>*´·tih*
31	**trettien**	*treht·tih·*<u>**eh**</u>*´n*
40	**førti**	*furr´·tih*
50	**femti**	<u>*fehm*</u>*´·tih*

60	**seksti** _sehks´·tih_
70	**sytti** _surt´·tih_
80	**åtti** _oht´·tih_
90	**nitti** _niht´·tih_
100	**hundre** _hewn`·druh_
101	**hundreogen** _hewn·druh·oh·**eh**´n_
200	**to hundre** _too hewn`·druh_
500	**fem hundre** _fehm hewn´·druh_
1,000	**tusen** _tew´·suhn_
10,000	**ti tusen** _tee tew´·suhn_
1,000,000	**en million** _ehn mihl·**yoo**´n_

Ordinal Numbers

first	**første** _furr`·stuh_
second	**andre** _ahn´·druh_
third	**tredje** _trehd´·yuh_
fourth	**fjerde** _fya`·ruh_
fifth	**femte** _fehm´·tuh_
once	**en gang** _ehn gahng_
twice	**to ganger** _too gahng`·uhr_
three times	**tre ganger** _treh gahng`·uhr_

Time

ESSENTIAL

What time is it?	**Hvor mye er klokken?** _voor **mui**´·uh ar klohk`·kuhn_
It's noon [midday].	**Den er tolv.** _dehn ar tohl_
At midnight.	**Ved midnatt.** _veh mihd´·naht_
From nine o'clock to five o'clock.	**Fra klokken ni til klokken fem.** _fra klohk`·kuhn n**ee** tihl klohk`·kuhn fehm_

Twenty after [past] four.	**Ti på halv fem.**	*tee poh hahl fehm*
A quarter to nine.	**Kvart på ni.**	*kvahrt poh nee*
5:30 a.m./p.m.	**Fem tretti/Sytten tretti.**	*fehm <u>treht´</u>•tih/<u>surt´</u>•tuhn <u>treht´</u>•tih*
Half past five.	**Halv seks.**	*hahl sehks*

Days

ESSENTIAL

Monday	**mandag**	<u>mahn´</u>•dahg
Tuesday	**tirsdag**	<u>teers´</u>•dahg
Wednesday	**onsdag**	<u>uns´</u>•dahg
Thursday	**torsdag**	<u>tawrs´</u>•dahg
Friday	**fredag**	<u>freh´</u>•dahg
Saturday	**lørdag**	<u>lurr´</u>•dahg
Sunday	**søndag**	<u>surn´</u>•dahg

Dates

yesterday	**i går**	*ih gawr*
today	**i dag**	*ih dahg*
tomorrow	**i morgen**	*ih <u>mawr`</u>•uhn*
day	**dag**	*dahg*
week	**uke**	<u>ew`</u>•kuh
month	**måned**	<u>maw`</u>•nuhd
year	**år**	*awr*

Months

January	**januar** yah·new·**ah**´r
February	**februar** feh·brew·**ah**´r
March	**mars** mahrs
April	**april** ahp·**ree**´l
May	**mai** mie
June	**juni** <u>yew</u>´·nee
July	**juli** <u>yew</u>´·lee
August	**august** ev·<u>gews</u>´t
September	**september** sehp·<u>tehm</u>´·buhr
October	**oktober** ohk·<u>taw</u>´·buhr
November	**november** nu·<u>vehm</u>´·buhr
December	**desember** deh·<u>sehm</u>´·buhr

Seasons

spring	**vår** vawr
summer	**sommer** <u>sohm</u>`·muhr
fall [autumn]	**høst** hurst
winter	**vinter** <u>vihn</u>´·tuhr

Major holidays in Norway include **Syttende mai** (Constitution Day, May 17), which is celebrated across the country with parades, flags, music, dance and other festivities. **Sankthansaften** (St. John's Eve), Midsummer Night, is the longest night of the year and is also a fun event, traditionally celebrated with bonfires.

Holidays

January 1	**Første nyttårsdag**	New Year's Day
May 1	**Første mai**	May Day (Labor Day)
May 17	**Syttende mai**	Constitution Day
December 25	**Første juledag**	Christmas Day
December 26	**Annen juledag**	Boxing Day

Moveable Dates

Maundy Thursday	**Skjærtorsdag**
Good Friday	**Langfredag**
Easter Sunday	**Første påskedag**
Easter Monday	**Annen påskedag**
Ascension Day	**Kristi himmelfartsdag**
Whit Sunday	**Første pinsedag**
Whit Monday	**Annen pinsedag**
St. John's Eve	**Sankthansaften**

Numerous festivals and cultural events are scheduled throughout the year in Norway, some with movable dates. Tourist offices, travel agencies, hotels and guidebooks offer extensive information about local and national celebrations. Many festivals are music oriented featuring folk, chamber and opera, with jazz music being especially popular.

Conversion Tables

When you know	Multiply by	To find
ounces	*28.3*	grams
pounds	*0.45*	kilograms
inches	*2.54*	centimeters
feet	*0.3*	meters
miles	*1.61*	kilometers
square inches	*6.45*	sq. centimeters
square feet	*0.09*	sq. meters
square miles	*2.59*	sq. kilometers
pints (U.S./Brit)	*0.47/0.56*	liters
gallons (U.S./Brit)	*3.8/4.5*	liters
Fahrenheit	*5/9, after 32*	Centigrade
Centigrade	*9/5, then +32*	Fahrenheit

Mileage

1 km	0.62 mi
5 km	3.10 mi
10 km	6.20 mi
20 km	12.4 mi
50 km	31.0 mi
100 km	62.0 mi

Measurement

1 gram	**et gram** *eht grahm*	= 0.035 oz.
1 kilogram (kg)	**et kilogram** *eht khee´·lu·grahm*	= 2.2 lb
1 liter (l)	**en liter** *ehn lee´·tuhr*	= 1.06 U.S./0.88 Brit. quarts

1 centimeter (cm)	**en centimeter**	= 0.4 inch
	ehn <u>sehn</u>´·tih·meh·tuhr	
1 meter (m)	**en meter** *ehn meh´·tuhr*	= 3.28 feet
1 kilometer (km)	**en kilometer**	= *0.62 mile*
	ehn khee´·lu·meh·tuhr	

Temperature

-40° C – -40° F	**5° C** – 41°F
-30° C – -22° F	**10° C** – 50° F
-20° C – -4° F	**15° C** – 59° F
-10° C – 14° F	**20° C** – 68° F
-5° C – 23° F	**25° C** – 77° F
-1° C – 30° F	**30° C** – 86° F
0° C – 32° F	**35° C** – 95° F

Oven Temperature

100° C – 212° F	**177° C** – 350° F
121° C – 250° F	**204° C** – 400° F
149° C – 300° F	**260° C** – 500° F

NORWEGIAN ALPHABET

Uppercase	Lowercase	Pronunciation as in
A	a	father
B	b	better
C	c	center
D	d	debt
E	e	entry
F	f	fine
G	g	get
H	h	hat
I	i	see
J	j	yes
K	k	kite
L	l	life
M	m	more
N	n	not
O	o	school
P	p	part
Q	q	quick
R	r	round
S	s	south
T	t	time
U	u	balloon
V	v	very
W	w	vine
X	x	x-ray
Y	y	entry
Z	z	some
Å	å	saw
Æ	æ	bat
Ø	ø	hurt

A

a (common nouns) en; **(neuter nouns)** et
access (internet) *v* bruke (internett)
accessories tilbehør
accident ulykke
accommodation innkvartering
account konto
acetaminophen paracetamol
acupuncture akupunktur
adapter adapter
address adresse
admission adgang
after etter
afternoon ettermiddag
air conditioning klimaanlegg
airline flyselskap
airmail luftpost
airport flyplass
aisle midtgang
aisle seat sete ved midtgangen
all alt
allergic allergisk
allergic reaction allergisk reaksjon

allowed tillatt
alter *v* endre
alternate route annen rute
aluminum foil aluminiumsfolie
amazing praktfull
ambulance sykebil
American *adj* amerikansk; *n* amerikaner
amusement park fornøyelsespark
anemic blodfattig
antibiotic antibiotikum
antique antikvitet
antiques store antikvitetshandel
antiseptic cream antiseptisk salve
any noe
anyone noen
anything noe
apartment leilighet
appetizer forrett
appointment avtale
arcade spillehall
area område
area code retningsnummer
aromatherapy aromaterapi
around (nearby) rundt

| **adj** adjective | **BE** British English | **prep** preposition |
| **adv** adverb | **n** noun | **v** verb |

arrival ankomst
arrive *v* komme frem
arthritis leddgikt
ask *v* spørre
aspirin aspirin
asthma astma
at ved
ATM minibank
attack overfall
attractive tiltrekkende
automatic *adj* automatisk

B

baby baby
baby bottle tåteflaske
baby wipes papirkluter
babysitter barnevakt
back *adv* (**direction**) tilbake;
  n (**body part**) rygg
backpack ryggsekk
bag (carrier) bærepose
baggage [BE] bagasje
baggage claim bagasjemottak
bakery bakeri
bandage bandasje
bank (finance) bank
bar (place) bar
barber herrefrisør
basket (store) handlekurv
basketball basketball
bathroom bad

battery batteri
battleground slagsted
be *v* være
beach strand
beautiful vakker
bed seng
before før
beginner begynner
behind bak
beige beige
belt belte
best best
bicycle sykkel
big stor
bike route sykkelsti
bikini bikini
bill regning
birthday fødselsdag
black svart
bland smakløs
blanket ullteppe
bleed *v* blø
blind blind
blood blod
blood pressure blodtrykk
blouse bluse
blue blå
boat båt
boarding ombordstigning
boarding pass
  ombordstigningskort

book bok
bookstore bokhandel
boot støvel
boring kjedelig
botanical gardens botanisk hage
bother v plage
bottle flaske
bottle opener flaskeåpner
bowl (container) bolle
boy gutt
boyfriend kjæreste
bra behå
bracelet armbånd
break down v (car) få motorstopp
breakfast frokost
breathe v puste
bridge bro
briefs underbukse
bring v (something) ta med
British britisk
broken (bone) brukket;
  (out of order) gått i stykker
brooch brosje
broom feiekost
brown brun
bug (insect) insekt
bus buss
bus station busstasjon
bus stop bussholdeplass
business forretning
business card visittkort

business center
  forretningssenter
busy opptatt
but men
buy v kjøpe; (treat) by på

C

cable car n taubane
cafe kafé
call n (phone) samtale;
  v (phone) ringe
camera kamera
camp v campe
campsite n campingplass
can v (be able to) kunne;
  n (container) boks
can opener boksåpner
cancel v annullere
candlestick lysestake
car bil
car hire [BE] bilutleie
car park [BE] parkeringsplass
car rental bilutleie
car seat barnesete
carafe karaffel
card kort
cardigan (Norwegian) lusekofte
carry v bære
carry-on (luggage)
  håndbagasje
cart (shopping) handlevogn;

(luggage) tralle
carton kartong
cash *v* løse inn; *n* kontanter
cashier kasse
castle slott
cathedral domkirke
cave hule
cell phone mobil
certificate of authenticity ekthetssertifikat
chair stol
chair lift stolheis
change *v* **(alter)** endre; **(baby)** bytte på; **(transport)** bytte; *v* **(money)** veksle; *n* **(money)** vekslepenger
cheap billig
check (payment) sjekk; **(restaurant)** regning
check in *v* **(airport)** sjekke inn
check-in desk innsjekkingsskranke
check out *v* sjekke ut
cheers skål
cheese slicer ostehøvel
chemical toilet kjemisk toalett
chemist [BE] apotek
cheque [BE] sjekk
chest bryst
chest pain vondt i brystet
chewing gum tyggegummi

child barn
children's menu barnemeny
children's portion barneporsjon
church kirke
cigar sigar
cigarette sigarett
cinema [BE] kino
city by
classical music klassisk musikk
clean *adj* ren; *v* vaske
cleaning supplies rengjøringsmidler
clear *v* **(ATM)** slette
cliff klippe
cling film [BE] plastfolie
close *v* stenge
closed stengt
clothing store klesbutikk
coat (man's) frakk; **(woman's)** kåpe
coin mynt
cold *adj* kald; *n* **(illness)** forkjølelse
colleague kollega
color farge
comb kam
come *v* komme
computer datamaskin
concert konsert
conditioner (hair) hårbalsam
condom kondom

conference konferanse
confirm v bekrefte
constipation forstoppelse
contact lens kontaktlinse
contact lens solution
  kontaktlinsevæske
convention hall
  konferansesenter
contain v inneholde
control n kontroll
cooking facilities
  kokemuligheter
copper kobber
corkscrew korketrekker
corner hjørne
cost v koste
cot [BE] (child's) sprinkelseng
cotton bomull
cough hoste
country land
country code landkode
countryside land
cover charge inngangspenger
cream (ointment) salve
credit card kredittkort
crib (child's) barneseng
crystal krystall
cup kopp
currency valuta
currency exchange office
  vekslingskontor

customs toll
cut v (with scissors) klippe
cute søt
cycling sykling
cycling race sykkelløp

D

dairy melkeprodukter
damage v skade
dance v danse
dance club diskotek
dark mørk
day dag
deaf døv
deck chair fluktstol
declare v (customs) fortolle
deep dyp
delay forsinkelse
delayed forsinket
delete v (computer) slette
delicatessen
  delikatesseforretning
denim dongeri
dentist tannlege
denture gebiss
deodorant deodorant
department store stormagasin
departure avgang
deposit (down payment)
  depositum
detergent vaskemiddel

diabetic diabetiker
diamond diamant
diaper bleie
diarrhea diarré
dictionary ordbok
diesel diesel
difficult vanskelig
digital digital
digital camera digitalkamera
digital photo digitalt bilde
digital print papirkopi av et digitalt bilde
dinner middag
direction retning
dirty skitten
disabled bevegelseshemmet
discount rabatt
dish *n* **(plate)** fat; **(food)** rett
dish detergent oppvaskmiddel
dishwasher oppvaskmaskin
display case monter
disposable camera engangskamera
disposable razor engangshøvel
dive *v* dykke
diving equipment dykkeutstyr
divorced skilt
dizzy svimmel
do *v* gjøre
doctor lege
dog hund

doll dukke
dollar dollar
domestic innenlands
door dør
double dobbel
double bed dobbeltseng
double room dobbeltrom
down ned
downtown sentrum
drag lift skitrekk
dress kjole
dress code kleskode
drink *v* drikke; *n* drikk
drink menu drikkekart
drive *v* kjøre
driver's license førerkort
driving licence [BE] førerkort
drop (liquid) dråpe
drowsiness søvnighet
dry tørr
dry cleaner renseri
dummy [BE] (baby's) narresmokk
duty (customs) toll
duty-free tollfri

E

earache øreverk
earring ørering
east øst
easy lett

eat v spise
economy class turistklasse
electrical outlet strømuttak
elevator heis
e-mail n **(message)** e-post;
  v sende e-post
e-mail address e-postadresse
emergency exit nødutgang
empty adj tom; v tømme
end n slutt; v slutte
English engelsk
English-speaking
  engelsktalende
engrave v gravere
enjoy v nyte
enter v gå inn
equipment utstyr
escalator rulletrapp
e-ticket e-billett
excess luggage overvektig bagasje
evening kveld
event begivenhet
exchange v veksle
exchange rate vekslingskurs
excursion utflukt
excuse v unnskylde
exit n utgang
expensive dyr
express ekspress
express mail ekspresspost
extension (phone) linje

extra ekstra
extra large ekstra stor
eye øye
eyebrow øyenbryn

F

face ansikt
facial ansiktsbehandling
family familie
fan (appliance) vifte
far langt
farm bondegård
fast hurtig
fax n faks; v fakse
fax number faksnummer
fee gebyr
feed v mate
ferry ferge
ferry landing fergested
fever feber
field jorde
fill (a prescription) v gjøre i stand
fill out v fylle ut
fill up v fylle
filling (tooth) plombe
fine (OK) bra
fire (open) ild; **(disaster)** brann
fire door branndør
first class første klasse
fit v passe
fitting room prøverom

fix *v* reparere
fjord fjord
flight flyavgang
floor etasje
flower blomst
folk music folkemusikk
food mat
foot fot
football [BE] fotball
football game [BE] fotballkamp
for for
forest skog
fork gaffel
form (document) skjema
formula morsmelkerstatning
fountain fontene
free fri
freezer fryser
fresh fersk
friend venn
from fra
frying pan stekepanne
full full
full time heltid

G

game (match) kamp
garbage bag søppelsekk
garden hage
gas (car) bensin
gas station bensinstasjon

gate utgang
get *v* **(find)** få tak i
get off *v* gå av
get to *v* komme til
gift gave
gift shop gavebutikk
girl jente
girlfriend kjæreste
give *v* gi
glacier bre
glass (drinking) glass
glasses (optical) briller
go *v* gå
go away *v* gå vekk
go out *v* gå ut
gold gull
golf golf
golf club golfkølle
golf course golfbane
golf tournament golfturnering
good god
good afternoon god dag
good evening god aften
good morning god morgen
good night god natt
goodbye adjø
gram gram
grandchild barnebarn
gray grå
green grønn
greeting hilsen

grocery store dagligvarebutikk
ground floor første etasje
guesthouse pensjonat
guide guide
guide dog førerhund
gym trimrom

H

hair hår
hair salon frisørsalong
hairbrush hårbørste
haircut klipp
hairdresser frisør
hairspray hårlakk
halal halal
half halv
handbag håndveske
handicapped handikappet
hard hard
hat hatt
have *v* ha
head hode
headache hodepine
health food store helsekostbutikk
health insurance sykeforsikring
hearing impaired hørselshemmet
heart hjerte
heart condition hjertesykdom
heat varme

heater varmeovn
heavy tung
heel hæl
hello hallo
helmet hjelm
help *n* hjelp; *v* (**assist**) hjelpe; (**oneself**) ta selv
here her
high høy
highchair babystol
highway motorvei
hill høyde
hire *n* utleie; *v* leie
hold on *v* (**phone**) vente litt
holiday helligdag; [BE] ferie
horse hest
hospital sykehus
hot varm
hotel hotell
hour time
house hus
how hvordan
how far hvor langt
how long hvor lenge
how late hvor sent
how many hvor mange
how much hvor mye
hungry sulten
hurry *n* hastverk
hurt *v* gjøre vondt
husband ektemann

I

I jeg
ibuprofen ibuprofen
icy kaldt
identification legitimasjon
ill [BE] syk
important viktig
impressive imponerende
in i
include v inkludere
indoor pool innendørs svømmebasseng
inexpensive rimelig
information informasjon
information desk informasjonsskranke
insect insekt
insect bite insektstikk
insect repellent insektmiddel
insert v sette inn
inside inni
instant messenger lynmelder
insurance forsikring
insurance claim forsikringskrav
interesting interessant
international internasjonal
internet internett
internet cafe internettkafé
interpreter tolk
intersection veikryss
introduce v (person)
presentere
iron (clothing) strykejern

J

jacket jakke
jazz jazz
jeans olabukse
jet-ski vannscooter
jeweler gullsmed
jewelry smykker
join v (go with somebody) bli med
just (only) bare

K

keep v beholde
key nøkkel
key card nøkkelkort
kiddie pool plaskebasseng
kilo kilo
kilometer kilometer
kiss v kysse
knife kniv
know v (something) vite; (somebody) kjenne
kosher koscher
krone (Norwegian currency) krone

L

lace knipling
lactose intolerant

laktoseintolerant
lake innsjø
language språk
large stor
last sist
late sen
later senere
launderette [BE]
 selvbetjeningsvaskeri
laundromat
 selvbetjeningsvaskeri
laundry (place) vaskeri;
 (clothes) vask
laundry facilities
 vaskemuligheter
lawyer advokat
leather lær
leave v **(depart)** dra;
 (deposit) legge igjen
leave alone v la være i fred
left (direction) venstre;
 (remaining) igjen
lens (for glasses) glass
less mindre
lesson time
letter brev
library bibliotek
life boat livbåt
life jacket flytevest
lifeguard badevakt
lift [BE] (elevator) heis

lift pass heiskort
light adj **(weight)** lett;
 adj **(color)** lys; n lys
light bulb lyspære
lighter lighter
like v like
line linje
linen (cloth) lin
liquor store vinmonopol
liter liter
little (some) litt
live v **(exist)** leve; **(reside)** bo
live music levende musikk
loafers mokkasiner
local lokal
lock lås
log in v logge seg inn
log off v logge seg av
log on v logge seg på
long lang
look n titt; v se
lose v miste
loud (voice) høy
love v elske
low lav
luggage bagasje
luggage cart bagasjetralle
luggage locker
 oppbevaringsboks
luggage trolley [BE] bagasjetralle
lunch lunsj

M

machine maskin
machine washable maskinvaskbar
magazine blad
magnificent storslagen
mail post
mailbox postkasse
make v lage
make up (a prescription) [BE] v gjøre i stand
mall kjøpesenter
man mann; **(gentleman)** herre
manager (shop) butikksjef
manicure manikyr
many mange
map kart
market marked
married gift
mass (church) messe
match (matchstick) fyrstikk; **(sport)** kamp
massage massasje
may (can) kunne
meal måltid
mean v bety
measuring cup målebeger
measuring spoon måleskje
medication legemiddel
medium mellomstor
meet v møtes

meeting møte
meeting room møterom
memory card minnebrikke
mend v lappe
menstrual cramps menstruasjonssmerter
menu meny
message beskjed
meter meter
microwave mikrobølgeovn
midday [BE] middag
midnight midnatt
mileage kjørelengde
minute minutt
miss v mangle
missing savnet
mistake feil
mobile (phone) mobil
moment øyeblikk
money penger
month måned
mop mopp
moped moped
more mer
morning morgen
mosque moské
motion sickness reisesyke
motorcycle motorsykkel
motorboat motorbåt
motorway [BE] motorvei
mountain fjell

mouth munn
move v flytte
movie film
movie theater kino
much mye
mug v overfalle
mugging overfall
museum museum
music musikk
must (have to) måtte

N

nail (human) negl
nail file neglefil
nail salon neglesalong
name navn
napkin serviett
nature preserve nasjonalpark
nauseous uvel
near nær
nearby i nærheten
necklace halskjede
need v trenge
new ny
newspaper avis
next neste
next to ved siden av
night natt
nightclub nattklubb
no nei; **(not anything)** ikke noe
no one ingen

non-alcoholic alkoholfri
non-carbonated kullsyrefri
non-smoking (area) for
  ikke-røykere
noon middag
north nord
Norway Norge
Norwegian n nordmann;
  adj norsk
not ikke
nothing ingenting
notify v underrette
novice nybegynner
now nå
number (shoes) nummer;
  (counting) tall
nurse sykepleier

O

off av
off-licence [BE] vinmonopol
office kontor
office hours kontortid
old gammel
on på
once én gang
one en
one-way ticket enveisbillett
only bare
open v åpne; adj åpen
opera opera

opposite midt imot
optician optiker
order v **(meal)** bestille
other andre
outdoor pool utendørs
  svømmebasseng
outlet (electric) stikkontakt
overlook utsikt
overnight natten over

P

p.m. (afternoon) om
  ettermiddagen; **(evening)** om
  kvelden
pacifier (baby's) narresmokk
pack v pakke
package pakke
paddling pool [BE]
  plaskebasseng
pain smerte
pajamas pyjamas
palace slott
pants langbukse
panty hose strømpebukse
paper papir
paper towel husholdningspapir
paracetamol [BE] paracetamol
park n park; v parkere
parking lot parkeringsplass
part time deltid
pass through v være på

gjennomreise
passport pass
passport control passkontroll
password passord
pastry bakverk
pastry shop konditori
path sti
pay v betale
peak topp
pearl perle
pediatrician barnelege
pedicure fotpleie
pen penn
penicillin penicillin
pensioner pensjonist
per day per dag
per hour per time
per kilometer per kilometer
per night per natt
per week per uke
perfume parfyme
period (menstruation)
  menstruasjon
permit v tillate
petrol [BE] bensin
petrol station [BE]
  bensinstasjon
pewter tinn
pharmacy apotek
phone telefon
phone call telefonsamtale

phone card telefonkort
phone number telefonnummer
photo foto
photocopy fotokopi
photograph fotografi
pick up *v* (person) hente
picnic picnic
picnic area turområde
piece stykke
pill pille; (contraceptive) p-pille
pillow pute
pink rosa
piste [BE] løype
piste map [BE] løypekart
place *n* (location) sted; (in hostel) plass
plaster [BE] (bandage) plaster
plastic wrap plastfolie
plate tallerken; (dessert) asjett
platform [BE] (station) perrong
play *n* (theatre) stykke; *v* spille
playground lekeplass
playing card spillkort
playpen lekegrind
please *adv* vær så snill
plunger klosettpumpe
pocket lomme
point *v* peke
point of interest severdighet
poles (ski) staver

police politi
police report politirapport
police station politistasjon
pond dam
pop music popmusikk
portion porsjon
possible mulig
post (mail) [BE] post
postage stamp frimerke
postbox [BE] postkasse
postcard postkort
post office postkontor
pound (British currency) pund
pregnant gravid
premium (gas) super
prepaid calling time ringetid
prescription resept
press *v* (iron) presse
pressure trykk
price pris
print *v* skrive ut; *n* (photo) kopi
problem problem
pronounce *v* uttale
pronunciation uttale
pull *v* trekke
purple fiolett
push *v* (open) skyve
pushchair [BE] gåstol
put *v* sette
put through sette over

Q

question spørsmål
quick rask
quickly øyeblikkelig
quiet rolig

R

racecourse [BE] travbane
racetrack travbane
racket (sport) racket
railway station [BE] jernbanestasjon
rain *n* regn; *v* regne
raincoat regnfrakk
rainy regnfull
rap (music) rap
rape voldtekt
rash utslett
rate (exchange) kurs
razor barberhøvel
razor blade barberblad
reach *v* nå
ready klar
real (genuine) ekte
receipt kvittering
receive *v* motta
recommend *v* anbefale
red rød
refrigerator kjøleskap
region område
regular (fuel) normalbensin

reindeer skin reinsdyrskinn
relationship forhold
rent *v* leie
rental car leiebil
repair *v* reparere
repeat gjenta
report *n* rapport; *v* **(a crime)** anmelde
reservation bestilling
reserve *v* bestille
restaurant restaurant
restroom toalett
retired (from work) pensjonert
return *v* **(come back)** komme tilbake; **(give back)** levere tilbake
return ticket [BE] tur-returbillett
right (correct) rett; **(direction)** høyre
ring (jewelry) ring
river elv
road vei
road map veikart
road sign trafikkskilt
rob rane
romantic romantisk
room rom
room service romservice
round (golf) runde
round-trip ticket tur-returbillett
route rute
rowboat robåt

rubbish [BE] søppel
rubbish bag [BE] søppelsekk
ruin ruin

S

safe *adj* **(free from danger)**
  trygg; *n* safe
sandals sandaler
sanitary napkin sanitetsbind
saucer skål
sauna badstue
save (computer) lagre
scarf skjerf
schedule (transport) rutetabell
scissors saks
sea sjø
sealskin slippers
  selskinnstøfler
seat plass
see *v* **(watch)** se; **(meet)**
  treffe; **(examine)** undersøke
sell *v* selge
seminar seminar
send *v* sende
senior citizen pensjonist
separately hver for seg
separated separert
sentence setning
serve *v* servere
service service; **(church)**
  gudstjeneste

shampoo sjampo
should burde
sheet laken
ship *n* skip; *v* sende
shirt skjorte
shoe store skobutikk
shoes sko
shop butikk
shopping area handlestrøk
shopping centre [BE]
  butikksenter
shopping mall butikksenter
shopping trolley [BE]
  handlevogn
short kort
shorts shorts
show *v* vise
shower dusj
shrine helligdom
sick (ill) syk
side side
side effect bivirkning
sightseeing sightseeing
sightseeing tour sightseeingtur
sign *v* undertegne
silk silke
silver sølv
single (unmarried) ugift
single room enkeltrom
single ticket [BE] enveisbillett
size (clothes) størrelse;

(shoes) nummer
ski v gå på ski
skis ski
ski lift skiheis
skirt skjørt
slice skive
slippers tøfler
slow langsom
slowly langsomt
small liten
smoke røyke
smoking (area) for røykere
sneakers turnsko
snorkeling equipment
  snorkleutstyr
snow n snø; v snø
snowboard snøbrett
snowshoes truger
soap såpe
soccer fotball
soccer game fotballkamp
sock sokk
someone noen
something noe
somewhere et eller annet sted
soon snart
sore throat sår hals
sorry v beklage
south sør
souvenir suvenir
souvenir store suvenirbutikk

spa spa
speak v snakke
speciality spesialitet
spoon skje
sports idrett
sports massage
  idrettsmassasje
sprained forstuet
square plass
stadium stadion
stairs trapp
stamp v stemple;
  n **(postage)** frimerke
start v starte
station stasjon
stay v **(remain)** bli; **(reside)** bo
steal v stjele
steep bratt
sterling silver sterlingsølv
stocking strømpe
stolen stjålet
stomach mage
stomachache magesmerte
stop n **(place)** holdeplass;
  v stoppe
store (shop) butikk
store directory butikkguide
stove komfyr
straight ahead rett frem
strange underlig
stream bekk

street gate
stroller gåstol
student student
study v studere
stunning overveldende
style v (hair) style
subway T-bane
subway station T-banestasjon
suit n (man's) dress;
  (woman's) drakt
suitable passende
suitcase koffert
sun sol
sunburn solforbrenning
sunglasses solbriller
sunscreen solkrem
sunstroke solstikk
super (gas) superbensin
supermarket supermarked
surfboard surfebrett
swallow v svelge
sweater genser
swelling hevelse
swim v svømme
swimming pool
  svømmebasseng
swimming trunks badebukse
swimsuit badedrakt
symbol tegn
synagogue synagoge

T

table bord
tablet (medical) tablett
take v ta
tampon tampong
taste v smake
tax skatt
taxi drosje
taxi rank [BE] drosjeholdeplass
taxi stand drosjeholdeplass
team lag
teaspoon teskje
tell v si
temple (religious) tempel
tennis tennis
tennis court tennisbane
tennis match tenniskamp
tent telt
terminal (airport) terminal
terrible forferdelig
text n tekst; v (message)
  tekste
than enn
thank v takke
theft tyveri
there (place) der;
  (direction) dit
these disse
thief tyv
thing ting
think v (believe) tro

this denne; dette
those de
throat hals
ticket billett
ticket office billettluke
tights [BE] strømpebukse
time (period) tid;
  (occasion) gang
timetable [BE] rutetabell
tissue papirlommetørkle
to (direction) til; **(time)** på
tobacco tobakk
tobacconist tobakkshandel
today i dag
toilet [BE] toalett
toilet paper toalettpapir
tomorrow i morgen
tonight i kveld
too for
tooth tann
toothache tannpine
toothbrush tannbørste
toothpaste tannpasta
tour tur
tourist office turistkontor
towel håndkle
town by
town map bykart
town square torg
toy leketøy
toy store leketøysbutikk

track (railway) spor
traditional tradisjonell
traffic light trafikklys
trail løype
trail map løypekart
train tog
train schedule togtabell
train station jernbanestasjon
tram trikk
translate v oversette
trash søppel
travel v reise
travel agency reisebyrå
travel guide reisehåndbok
travel sickness reisesyke
traveler's check reisesjekk
trim (hair) stuss
trip tur
troll troll
trousers [BE] langbukse
try on v prøve
T-shirt T-skjorte
turn off (device) skru av
turn on (device) skru på
TV TV
type v **(computer)** skrive
typically typisk

U

ugly stygg
umbrella paraply

underground [BE] *n* T-bane
underground station [BE]
  T-banestasjon
undershirt trøye
understand *v* forstå
unleaded blyfri
until til
upset stomach urolig mage
use *n* bruk; *v* bruke
username brukernavn

V

vacation ferie
vacuum cleaner støvsuger
vaginal infection
  underlivsbetennelse
valley dal
value verdi
VAT [BE] moms
vegetarian vegetarianer
very meget
viking ship vikingskip
visit *n* besøk; *v* **(a person)**
  besøke
visiting hours besøkstid
visually impaired synshemmet
volleyball game volleyballkamp
vomit *v* kaste opp

W

wait *v* vente

waiter servitør
waitress servitør
wake *v* vekke
wake-up call vekking
walk *v* **(go)** gå; **(stroll)** spasere
wallet lommebok
want *v* ville
warm *adj* varm; *v* varme
wash *v* vaske
washable vaskbar
washing mashine vaskemaskin
watch klokke
water vann
waterfall foss
water skis vannski
weather vær
weather forecast værutsikter
week uke
weekend helg
welcome velkommen
west vest
what hva
wheelchair rullestol
wheelchair ramp
  rullestolsrampe
when når
where hvor
which hvilken
white hvit
who hvem
whole hel

widowed (man) enkemann;
  (woman) enke
wife kone
window vindu
window seat vindusplass
windsurfer seilbrett
wine list vinkart
wireless internet trådløst internett
with med
withdraw *v* **(from account)**
  ta ut
without uten
woman kvinne
wooden figurine trefigur
wool ull
work *v* **(toil)** arbeide;
  (function) virke
wrap up *v* pakke inn
write *v* skrive
wrong i veien

Y

year år
yellow gul
yes ja
yesterday i går
you du
youth hostel vandrerhjem

Z

zoo dyrehage

Norwegian–English Dictionary

A

adapter adapter
adjø goodbye
adresse address
advokat lawyer
akkurat nå right now
akupunktur acupuncture
alkoholfri non-alcoholic
allergisk allergic
allergisk reaksjon allergic reaction
alt all
aluminiumsfolie aluminum foil
amerikaner *n* American
amerikansk *adj* American
anbefale *v* recommend
andre other
ankomst arrival
anmelde *v* report (a theft)
annen rute alternate route
annullere *v* cancel
ansikt face
ansiktsbehandling facial
antibiotikum antibiotic
antikvitet antique
antikvitetshandel antiques store
antiseptisk salve antiseptic cream
aperitiff aperitif
apotek pharmacy [chemist BE]
arbeide *v* work

armbånd bracelet
aromaterapi aromatherapy
asjett plate (dessert)
aspirin aspirin
astma asthma
automatisk automatic
av off
avgang departure
avis newspaper
avtale appointment

B

baby baby
babystol highchair
bad bathroom
badebukse swimming trunks
badedrakt swimsuit
badevakt lifeguard
badstue sauna
bagasje luggage [baggage BE]
bagasjemottak baggage claim
bagasjetralle luggage cart [trolley BE]
bak behind
bakeri bakery
bakverk pastry
bandasje bandage
bank bank (finance)
bar *n* bar (place)

barberblad razor blade
barberhøvel razor
bare just; only
barn child
barnebarn grandchild
barnelege pediatrician
barnemeny children's menu
barneporsjon children's portion
barnesete car seat
barnevakt babysitter
basketball basketball
batteri battery
be om v ask for
begivenhet event
begynner beginner
beholde v keep
behå bra
beige beige
bekk stream
beklage v be sorry
bekrefte v confirm
belte belt
bensin gas [petrol BE] (car)
bensinstasjon gas [petrol BE] station
beskjed message
best best
bestille v order (meal); reserve
bestilling reservation
besøk n visit
besøke v visit (someone)

besøkstid visiting hours
betale v pay
bety v mean
bevegelseshemmet disabled
bibliotek library
bikini bikini
bil car
billett ticket
billettluke ticket office
billig cheap
bilutleie car rental [hire BE]
bivirkning side effect
blad magazine
bleie diaper
bli v stay (remain)
bli med v join (someone)
blind blind
blod blood
blodfattig anemic [anaemic BE]
blodtrykk blood pressure
blomst flower
bluse blouse
blyfri unleaded
blø v bleed
blå blue
bo live (reside); stay (reside)
bok book
bokhandel bookstore
boks can (container)
boksåpner can opener

bolle bowl
bomull cotton
bondegård farm
bord table
botanisk hage botanical gardens
bra fine (OK)
brann fire (disaster)
branndør fire door
bratt steep
bre glacier
brev letter
briller glasses
britisk British
bro bridge
brosje brooch
bruk *n* use
bruke *v* use
brukernavn username
brukket broken (bone)
brun brown
bryst chest
burde should
buss bus
bussholdeplass bus stop
busstasjon bus station
butikk store [shop BE]
butikkguide store directory
butikksenter shopping mall
  [centre BE]
butikksjef manager (shop)
by *n* city; town

bykart town map
bytte *v* change (transportation)
bytte på *v* change (baby)
bære *v* carry
bærepose bag (carrier)
båt boat

C

campe *v* camp
camping camping
campingplass campsite

D

dag day
dagligvarebutikk grocery store
dal valley
dam pond
danse *v* dance
dansk Danish
datamaskin computer
delikatesseforretning
  delicatessen
deltid part time
denne this
deodorant deodorant
depositum deposit
  (down payment)
der there (place)
dette this
diabetiker diabetic
diamant diamond

diarré diarrhea
die breastfeed
diesel diesel
digital digital
digitalkamera digital camera
digitalt bilde digital photo
diskotek dance club
disse these
dit there (direction)
dobbel double
dobbeltrom double room
dobbeltseng double bed
dollar dollar
domkirke cathedral
dongeri denim
dra v leave (depart)
drakt suit (woman's)
dress suit (man's)
drikk n drink
drikke v drink
drikkekart drink menu
drosje taxi
drosjeholdeplass taxi stand [rank BE]
dråpe drop (liquid)
du you
dukke doll
dusj shower
dykke v dive
dykkeutstyr diving equipment
dyp adj deep

dyr adj expensive
dyrehage zoo
dør door
døv deaf

E

e-billett e-ticket
ekspert expert
ekspress express
ekspresspost express mail
ekstra extra
ekstra stor extra large
ekte real (genuine)
ektemann husband
ekthetssertifikat certificate of authenticity
elske v love
elv river
en a (common nouns); one
endre v change
engangshøvel disposable razor
engangskamera disposable camera
engelsk English
engelsktalende English-speaking
enke widowed (woman)
enkeltrom single room
enkemann widowed (man)
enn than
enveisbillett one-way

[single BE] ticket
e-post e-mail
e-postadresse e-mail addess
erfaren experienced
et a (neuter nouns)
et eller annet sted somewhere
et øyeblikk hold on (phone)
etasje floor
etter after
ettermiddag afternoon

F

faks *n* fax
fakse *v* fax
faksnummer fax number
familie family
farge color
fat dish
feber fever
feiekost broom
feil mistake
ferge ferry
ferie vacation [holiday BE]
fersk fresh
film movie
fiolett purple
fjell mountain
fjord fjord
flaske bottle
flaskeåpner bottle opener
fluktstol deck chair

fly flight
flyplass airport
flyselskap airline
flytevest life jacket
flytte *v* move
folkemusikk folk music
fontene fountain
for for; too
for røykere smoking (area)
forferdelig terrible
forhold relationship
forkjølelse cold (illness)
fornøyelsespark amusement park
forretning business
forretningssenter business center
forrett appetizer
forsikring insurance
forsikringskrav insurance claim
forsinkelse delay
forsinket delayed
forstoppelse constipation
forstuet sprained
forstå *v* understand
fortolle *v* declare (customs)
foss waterfall
fot foot
fotball soccer [football BE]
fotballkamp soccer
 [football BE] game
foto photo
fotokopi photocopy

fotpleie pedicure
fra from
frakk coat (man's)
fri free
frimerke stamp (postage)
frisør hairdresser
frisørsalong hair salon
frokost breakfast
fryser freezer
full full
fylle *v* fill up
fylle ut *v* fill out
fyrstikk match (matchstick)
fødselsdag birthday
før before
førerhund guide dog
førerkort driver's license
  [driving licence BE]
første etasje ground floor
første klasse first class
få motorstopp *v* break down (car)
få tak i *v* get (find)

G

gaffel fork
gammel old
gang time (occasion)
gate street
gave gift
gavebutikk gift shop
gebiss denture

gebyr fee
genser sweater
gi *v* give
gift *adj* married
gir *n* speed (cycle)
gjenta *v* repeat
gjøre *v* do
gjøre i stand *v* make up (prepare)
gjøre vondt *v* hurt
glass glass (drinking)
glass lens (for glasses)
god good
god aften good evening
god dag good afternoon
god morgen good morning
god natt good night
godter candy
golf golf
golfbane golf course
golfkølle golf club
golfturnering golf tournament
gram gram
gravere *v* engrave
gravid pregnant
gryte pot
grå gray
grønn green
gudstjeneste service (church)
guide guide
gul *adj* yellow
gull *n* gold

gullsmed jeweler
gult gull yellow gold
gutt boy
gå v go; walk
gå av v get off
gå inn v enter
gå på ski v ski
gå seg bort v get lost
gå ut v go out
gå vekk go away
gåstol stroller [pushchair, buggy BE]
gått i stykker broken
(out of order)

H

ha v have
ha det travelt v be in a hurry
ha gått seg bort v be lost
hage garden
halal halal
hallo hello
hals throat
halskjede necklace
halv half
halvtime half an hour
handikappet handicapped
handlekurv basket (shopping)
handlestrøk shopping area
handlevogn shopping cart
[trolley BE]
hans his

hard hard
haste v to be urgent
hatt hat
heis elevator [lift BE]
heiskort lift pass
hel whole
helg weekend
helligdag holiday
helligdom shrine
helsekostbutikk health food store
heltid full time
hennes her
hente v pick up (person)
her here
herre man (gentleman)
herrefrisør barber
hest horse
hevelse swelling
hilsen greeting
hjelm helmet
hjelp n help
hjelpe v help
hjerte heart
hjertesykdom heart condition
hjørne corner
hode head
hodepine headache
holde rundt hug
holdeplass stop (place)
hoste v cough
hotell hotel

hule *n* cave
hullsleiv spatula
hund dog
hurtig fast
hus house
husholdningspapir paper towel
hva what
hvem who
hver for oss separately
hvilken which
hvit white
hvitt gull white gold
hvor where
hvor langt how far
hvor lenge how long
hvor mange how many
hvor mye how much
hvor sent how late
hvordan how
hæl heel
hørselshemmet hearing impaired
høy high (tall); loud (voice)
høyde hill
høyre right (direction)
håndbagasje carry-on (luggage)
håndkle towel
håndveske handbag
hår hair
hårbalsam conditioner (hair)
hårbørste hairbrush
hårlakk hair spray

I

i in
i dag today
i går yesterday
i kveld tonight
i morgen tomorrow
i nærheten nearby
i veien wrong
ibuprofen ibuprofen (pharmaceutical)
idrett sports
idrettsmassasje sports massage
igjen left (remaining)
ikke not
ikke noe no (not anything)
ild fire (open)
imponerende impressive
informasjon information
informasjonsskranke information desk
ingen no one
ingenting nothing
inkludere *v* include
inkludert included
inneholde *v* contain
innendørs svømmebasseng indoor pool
innenlands domestic
inngangsbillett admission (price)
inngangspenger cover charge
inni inside

innkvartering accommodations
[accomodation BE]
innsjekkingsskranke check-in
innsjø lake
insekt insect, bug
insektmiddel insect repellent
insektstikk insect bite
interessant interesting
interessert interested
internasjonal international
internett internet
internettkafé internet cafe

J

ja yes
jakke jacket
jazz jazz
jeg I
jente girl
jernbanestasjon train
[railway BE] station
jorde field

K

kafé cafe
kald cold
kaldt icy
kam comb
kamera camera
kamp game; match (sport)
karaffel carafe

kart map
kartong carton
kasse cash desk
kaste opp v vomit
kelner waiter
kilo kilo
kilometer kilometer
[kilometre BE]
kino movie theater [cinema BE]
kirke church
kjedelig boring
kjemisk toalett chemical toilet
kjenne v know (somebody)
kjole dress
kjæreste boyfriend; girlfriend
kjøleskap refrigerator
kjøpe buy
kjøpesenter mall
kjøre v drive
kjørelengde mileage
klar ready
klassisk musikk classical music
klesbutikk clothing store
kleskode dress code
klimaanlegg air conditioning
klipp haircut
klippe n cliff; v cut
(with scissors)
klokke watch
klosettpumpe plunger
knipling lace

kniv knife
kobber copper
koffert suitcase
kokemuligheter cooking facilities
kollega colleague
komfyr stove
komme v come
komme frem v arrive
komme til v get to
komme tilbake v return
  (come back)
konditori pastry shop
kondom condom
kone wife
konferanse conference
konferansesenter convention hall
konsert concert
kontaktlinse contact lens
kontaktlinsevæske contact lens
  solution
kontanter cash
konto account
kontor office
kontortid office hours
kontroll control
kopi print (photo)
kopp cup
korketrekker corkscrew
kort n card; adj short
koscher kosher
koste v cost

kredittkort credit card
krone krone
  (Norwegian currency)
krystall crystal
kullsyrefri non-carbonated [still
  BE] (drink)
kunne can; may
kurs rate (of exchange)
kveld evening
kvinne woman
kvittering receipt
kysse v kiss
kåpe coat (woman's)

L

la oss let's
la være i fred v leave alone
lag team
lage v make
lagre v save (computer)
laken sheet
laktoseintolerant lactose
  intolerant
land country; countryside
landekode country code
lang long
langbukser pants
  [trousers BE]
langsom slow
langsomt slowly
langt far

lappe v mend
lav low
lavhælt flat (shoe)
leddgikt arthritis
lege doctor
legemiddel medication
legge igjen v leave (deposit)
legitimasjon identification
leie v hire; rent
leiebil rental car
leilighet apartment
lekegrind playpen
lekeplass playground
leketøy toy
leketøysbutikk toy store
lett easy; light (weight)
leve v live
levende musikk live music
levere tilbake v return
  (give back)
lighter lighter
like v like
lin linen (cloth)
linje line (transport); extension
  (phone)
liten small
liter liter
litt little; some
  (with singular nouns)
livbåt life boat
logge seg av log off

logge seg inn log in
logge seg på log on
lokal local
lomme pocket
lommebok wallet
lunsj lunch
lusekofte cardigan (Norwegian)
lynmelder instant messenger
lys n light; adj light (color)
lysestake candlestick
lyspære light bulb
lær leather
løse inn v cash
løype trail [piste BE]
løypekart trail map
  [piste map BE]
lås lock
låse seg ute v lock oneself out

M

mage stomach
magesmerte stomachache
mange many
mangle v miss
manikyr manicure
mann man
marked market
maskin machine
maskinvaskbar machine washable
massasje massage
mat food

mate *v* feed
med with
meget very
melkeprodukter dairy
mellomstor medium
men but
menstruasjon period (monthly)
menstruasjonssmerter
  menstrual cramps
meny menu
mer more
messe mass (church)
meter meter
middag dinner (meal); noon
  [midday BE]
midnatt midnight
midt imot opposite
midtgang aisle
mikrobølgeovn microwave
mindre less
minibank ATM
minnebrikke memory card
minutt minute
miste *v* lose
mobil cell [mobile BE] phone
mokkasiner loafers
moms sales tax [VAT BE]
monter display case
moped moped
mopp mop
morgen morning

morsmelkerstatning formula
moské mosque
motorbåt motorboat
motorsykkel motorcycle
motorvei highway
  [motorway BE]
motta *v* receive
mulig possible
munn mouth
museum museum
musikk music
mye much
mynt coin
mørk dark
møte meeting
møterom meeting room
møtes *v* meet
målebeger measuring cup
måleskje measuring spoon
måltid meal
måned month
måtte *v* must (have to)

N

narresmokk pacifier
  [dummy BE] (baby's)
nasjonalpark nature preserve
natt night
natten over overnight
nattklubb nightclub
navn name

ned down
negl nail (human)
neglefil nail file
neglesalong nail salon
nei no
neste next
noe any; anything; something
noen anyone; some (with plural nouns); someone
nord north
Norge Norway
normalbensin regular (fuel)
norsk Norwegian
nummer number (counting); size (shoes)
ny new
nybegynner novice
nyte *v* enjoy
nær near
nærmeste nearest
nødutgang emergency exit
nøkkel key
nøkkelkort key card
nå *adv* now; *v* reach
når when

O

olabukser jeans
om ettermiddagen p.m. (afternoon)
om kvelden p.m. (evening)

om morgenen a.m.
ombordstigning boarding
ombordstigningskort boarding pass
område area; region
opera opera
oppbevaringsboks luggage locker
opptatt busy
oppvaskmaskin dishwasher
oppvaskmiddel dish detergent [washing-up liquid BE]
optiker optician
ordbok dictionary
ostehøvel cheese slicer
overfall attack; mugging
overfalle *v* mug
oversette *v* translate
overvektig bagasje excess luggage
overveldende stunning

P

p-pille pill (contraceptive)
pakke package [parcel BE]; *v* pack
pakke inn *v* wrap up
palass palace
papir paper
papirkluter baby wipes
papirkopi av et digitalt bilde digital print

papirlommetørkle tissue
paracetamol acetaminophen
  [paracetamol BE]
paraply umbrella
parfyme perfume
parfymeri perfumery
park *n* park
parkere *v* park
parkeringsplass parking lot
  [car park BE]
pass passport
passe *v* fit
passende suitable
passkontroll passport control
passord password
peke *v* point
penger money
penicillin penicillin
penn pen
pensjonat guesthouse
pensjonert retired (from work)
pensjonist senior citizen
per dag per day
per kilometer per kilometer
  [kilometre BE]
per natt per night
per time per hour
per uke per week
perle pearl
perrong platform [BE] (station)
picnic picnic

pille pill
plage *v* bother
plaskebasseng kiddie
  [paddling BE] pool
plass place (hostel); seat; square
plaster bandage [plaster BE]
plastfolie plastic wrap
  [cling film BE]
plombe filling (tooth)
politi police
politirapport police report
politistasjon police station
popmusikk pop music
porsjon portion
post mail [post BE]
postkasse mailbox [postbox BE]
postkontor post office
postkort postcard
praktfull amazing
presentere *v* introduce (person)
presse *v* press (iron)
pris price
problem problem
protestantisk Protestant
prøve *v* try on
prøverom fitting room
pund pound (money)
puste *v* breathe
pute pillow
pyjamas pajamas
på on (place); to (time)

R

rabatt discount
racket racket (sport)
rane rob
rap rap (music)
rapport report
rask quick
regn n rain
regne v rain
regnfrakk raincoat
regnfull rainy
regning n check [bill BE]
  (restaurant)
reinsdyrskinn reindeer skin
reise v travel
reisebyrå travel agency
reisehåndbok travel guide
reisesjekk traveler's check
  [cheque BE]
reisesyke motion sickness
ren clean
rengjøringsmidler cleaning
  supplies
renseri dry cleaner
reparere v fix; repair
resept prescription
restaurant restaurant
retning direction
retningsnummer area code
rett dish (food); right (correct)
rett frem straight ahead

rimelig inexpensive
ring n ring (jewelry)
ringe v call (phone)
ringetid prepaid calling time
robåt rowboat
rolig quiet
rom room
romantisk romantic
romservice room service
rosa pink
ruin n ruin
rullestol wheelchair
rullestolsrampe wheelchair ramp
rulletrapp escalator
runde round (golf)
rundt around (nearby)
rute route
rutetabell schedule
  [timetable BE] (transportation)
rygg back (body part)
ryggsekk backpack
rød red
røyke v smoke
røykfri non-smoking (area)

S

safe n safe; adj trygg
saks scissors
salve cream (pharmaceutical)
samtale call (phone)
sandaler sandals

sanitetsbind sanitary napkin [towel BE]

savnet missing

se v look; see

seilbrett windsurfer

selge v sell

selvbetjeningsvaskeri laundromat [launderette BE]

seminar seminar

sen late

sende v send; ship

sende e-post v e-mail

senere later

seng bed

sentrum downtown area

separert separated

servere v serve

service service

serviett napkin

servitør waiter, waitress

sete ved midtgangen aisle seat

setning sentence

sette v put

sette inn v insert

sette over v put through

severdighet point of interest

shorts shorts

si v tell

side side

sigar cigar

sigarett cigarette

sightseeing sightseeing

sightseeingtur sightseeing tour

silke silk

sist last

sjampo shampoo

sjekk n check [cheque BE]

sjekke e-post v check e-mail

sjekke inn check in (airport)

sjekke ut check out

sjø sea

skade v damage

skatt tax

ski skis

skiheis ski lift

skilt divorced

skip ship

skitrekk drag lift

skitten dirty

skive slice

skje spoon

skjema form (document)

skjerf scarf

skjorte shirt

skjørt skirt

sko shoes

skobutikk shoe store

skog forest

skrive v write; type (computer)

skrive ut v print

skru av v turn off (device)

skru på v turn on (device)

skyve *v* push (open)
skål saucer; cheers (a toast)
slagsted battleground
sleiv spatula
slett *v* clear (ATM)
slette *v* delete (computer)
slott castle
slutt *n* end
slutte *v* end
smake *v* taste
smakløs bland
smerte pain
smykker jewelry
snakke *v* speak
snart soon
snorkleutstyr snorkeling equipment
snø *n/v* snow
snøbrett snowboard
sokk sock
sol sun
solbriller sunglasses
solforbrenning sunburn
solkrem sunscreen
solstikk sunstroke
sommer summer
spa spa
spasere *v* walk (stroll)
spesialitet speciality
spille *v* play
spille på hester *v* place a bet

spillehall arcade
spillkort playing card
spise *v* eat
spisekart menu (printed)
spor track (railway)
springvann tap water
sprinkelseng crib [child's cot BE]
språk language
spørre *v* ask
spørsmål question
stadion stadium
starte *v* start
stasjon station
staver poles (ski)
sted place
stekepanne frying pan
stemple stamp
stenge *v* close
stengt closed
sterlingsølv sterling silver
sti path
stikkontakt outlet (electric) [socket BE]
stjele *v* steal
stjålet stolen
stol chair
stolheis chair lift
stoppe *v* stop
stor big; large
stormagasin department store

storslagen magnificent
strand beach
strykejern iron (clothing)
strømpe stocking
strømpebukse panty hose [tights BE]
strømuttak electrical outlet
student student
studere v study
stuss trim (hair)
stygg ugly
stykke piece; play (theater)
style v style (hair)
større bigger
størrelse size (clothes)
støvel boot
støvsuger vacuum cleaner
sulten hungry
super premium; super (gasoline)
supermarked supermarket
surfebrett surfboard
surstoffbehandling oxygen treatment
suvenir souvenir
suvenirbutikk souvenir store
svart black
svelge v swallow
svensk Swedish
Sverige Sweden
svimmel dizzy
svømme v swim

svømmebasseng swimming pool
syk sick [ill BE]
sykebil ambulance
sykeforsikring health insurance
sykehus hospital
sykepleier nurse
sykkel bicycle
sykkelløp cycling race
sykkelsti bike route
sykling cycling
synagoge synagogue
synshemmet visually impaired
sølv silver
søppel trash [rubbish BE]
søppelsekk garbage [rubbish BE] bag
sør south
søt cute
søvnighet drowsiness
såpe soap
sår hals sore throat

T

T-bane subway [underground BE]
T-banestasjon subway [underground BE] station
T-skjorte T-shirt
ta v take
ta med v bring (something)
ta med seg v take away (carry)

Berlitz®

speaking your language

phrase book & dictionary
phrase book & CD

Available in: Arabic, Brazilian Portuguese*, Burmese*, Cantonese
Chinese, Croatian, Czech*, Danish*, Dutch, English, Filipino, Finnish*, French,
German, Greek, Hebrew*, Hindi*, Hungarian*, Indonesian, Italian, Japanese,
Korean, Latin American Spanish, Malay, Mandarin Chinese, Mexican Spanish,
Norwegian, Polish, Portuguese, Romanian*, Russian, Spanish, Swedish, Thai,
Turkish, Vietnamese
*Book only